Jeff Burroughs'
Little League
Instructional Guide

Jeff Burroughs

Bonus Books, Inc., Chicago

98 97 96 95 94   5 4 3 2 1

Library of Congress Catalog Card Number: 94-70386

International Standard Book Number: 1-56625-009-9

Bonus Books, Inc.
160 East Illinois Street
Chicago, Illinois 60611

First Edition

*Front cover photo of Ryan Beaver courtesy of Alex Garcia /
Press-Telegram.*

Typesetting by Point West, Inc., Carol Stream, IL

Printed in the United States of America

Contents

Introduction

I remember when I was a kid and my friends and I would play little pick-up games of baseball down the street from my house at Stearns Park, in Long Beach, California. We used to pretend that we were up at bat with the bases loaded, two outs in the bottom of the sixth inning in the championship Little League game in Williamsport, Pennsylvania. We used to talk about Williamsport all the time, even though we didn't have the vaguest idea where Williamsport actually was. All we knew was that was where they held the Little League world championships every year and one day we would be there.

We never did get there, not as children anyway. But in the summer of 1992 and then again in 1993, I made it as a coach with the Long Beach Little League All-Star team with my son, Sean. I have to admit, I was probably more excited than any of the children during both years. My lifelong dream had finally come true. It took me 40 years, but I finally got to be on that most hallowed of all baseball fields, the one in Williamsport, Pennsylvania.

◆

My lifelong love of baseball began 42 years ago in Long Beach, California. I was born March 7, 1951, the only son of Charles and Iona Burroughs. I grew up playing in the exact same park and Little League that all my children ended up playing in, Long Beach Little League at Stearns Park. I played Little League, Pony League, Colt League, American Legion and high school baseball at Wilson High School in Long Beach.

My Little League All-Star team was defeated and eliminated in three games in 1963 because the coach opted to pitch the president of the League's son instead of our star pitcher. You never get over those memories. At 13 and 14, I played in Pony League and in 1965, our Pony League team won the United States National Title. I will never forget that summer.

I played baseball at Wilson High School and was drafted as the number one pick in the entire nation in the free agent draft by the Washington Senators when I was a senior.

I began my career in Wytheville, Virginia, and moved on in 1970 to Triple A ball in Denver, Colorado, before finally getting a chance to play in the major leagues with the Texas Rangers baseball team. In 1974, I was named the American League's Most Valuable Player and the *Sporting News* Player of the Year. I was traded in 1978 to the Atlanta Braves. I also played for the Seattle Mariners in 1981 and for the Oakland A's in 1982 through 1984. I ended my career with the Toronto Blue Jays in 1985, the year that they won the Eastern division championship for the first time.

My wife and I came back home to Long Beach with three young children in tow: Scott, 6, Sean, 4, and Shaelen, 1. Scott was just beginning to play tee ball, and we used to go out there and support him as he played the game his dad had played for so long. At this point in time, I had no desire to be a coach. I just wanted to spend my time in the stands cheering my kids on.

◆

One day, the coach of my son's team could not make it to a game because of a business trip. I volunteered to help out and went onto the field. There I was in the midst of 14 screaming, hyperactive six- and seven-year-olds. I had no idea what to do next, so I sort of blended in with the rest of the kids hoping I would get out alive. In the fifth inning, a small kid named Jimmy came back to the dugout crying after another unsuccessful time at bat. I remarked to him that he wasn't standing correctly up at home plate and he was holding his hands wrong. I gave him a few tips. He shook his head and said that he would give them a try. The next time at bat, Jimmy went up to the tee and hit the hardest line drive he had ever hit in his life. The ball screamed past the outfielders and Jimmy ran all the way around the bases for a home run. He came back to the dugout with the biggest smile on his face and told me, "Thanks, coach, what you told me really worked well."

Right then and there, it happened. I was hooked. Little did I know that from that day on my future would be jammed with eight years of practices, car pools, tournaments, games, dealing with parents and everything else that goes along with being a coach. And I have to say that those eight years have been the most fun, exciting, poignant, dramatic, worthwhile and gratifying years I have spent on this planet.

After that day with Jimmy, I went on to coach my kids in Little League beginning with tee ball, then the Minor B's, Minor A's, Major League and All-Star play. We won championships in tee ball, Minor B, Minor A, Major League, a district title (for the first time in 42 years in Long Beach Little League) and two Little League World Championships. Even more important than winning, the kids had a fabulous time, and I hope I did my part in providing them with the help they needed to learn the game of baseball and how to conduct themselves properly. I really hope I can be one of the people these kids will remember. When they get older maybe

◆

they'll say, "My coach in Little League was the first one to get me to understand how much fun baseball can really be." I believe that is the real reason why all of us coaches coach.

After our World Series victory last year, I had a few weeks to reflect on how blessed I was to be able to coach and have that special relationship not only with my kids but with all of the little ballplayers I have taught over the years. I would not trade those years for anything. I began to wonder, why wouldn't all parents want to get involved during those special years when their kids are growing up?

The only answer I could come up with was that maybe a lot of adults don't feel that they are qualified to run a youth baseball team, that they know enough about baseball to really give the children what they need.

The purpose of this book is to help you solve that problem by providing you with enough knowledge about baseball and some proven baseball methods that you can use to get the most out of your coaching experience. As you read, you'll note that I usually refer to players as "he." That's just to keep it simple, and I hope the many talented girls playing on teams across the country will understand.

The suggestions in this book are exactly the same methods that we use to instruct our kids. If you stay within the framework that is outlined here in this book, I guarantee that you will have a tremendously rewarding time coaching youth baseball.

In 1993 there were 19 million young people playing baseball in the United States. We need all the adults we can find to really give something back to these kids and to provide leadership and role models for our future generations.

I hope this book will give you some help in coaching kids in this great game of ours.

Play ball.

◆

Hitting

Hitting a baseball has often been called the most difficult thing to do in sports, and with good reason. You are trying to hit a round object with a round bat coming at you at a high speed. No wonder it is so difficult. A hitter is considered a success on any level in baseball if he can hit .300. That's three hits out of 10 times at bat, so you can fail 70% of the time and still be considered a star. A .300 hitter in the majors today would be worth three million a year.

No other exercise in sports is more fun than hitting a baseball. I remember during my playing career I went early to the ballpark and watched grown men take batting practice. At the end of the warm-ups I could see the players literally fighting to get in the batting cage and get in those last few swings before the groundskeepers took the cages away. Hitting is fun, no matter how old you are.

In this book, we will try to explain the basics of coaching youth baseball. Then any coach or parent across the country can read this and teach hitting a baseball to children knowing that what you are teaching is the correct way.

◆

I have been in amateur baseball for eight years now, and I always marvel that people can hold practices and let children play and practice the wrong way. I firmly believe that if you are going to coach a team, you should know the correct way of teaching in order to build a solid baseball foundation that the kids will understand and use for the rest of their baseball careers. Once this happens and the children start having some success, they will get more enjoyment out of the game.

The Bat

This is as good a place to start as any. I will talk a lot about being comfortable and balanced before, during and after the actual baseball swing, and it all begins, obviously, with the bat.

The single most common mistake players make when choosing a bat is a result of the Superman complex that a lot of kids seem to have. That is, the bigger and longer a bat is, the better a hitter that person should be. I've never understood that way of thinking. People actually think that a huge, heavy cumbersome piece of pine will somehow have a magic radar that will lead the bat to the baseball more easily than a light bat would. Remember, if you are going to be a good hitter, you have to feel comfortable and have good balance. A telephone pole in your hands will not do the job. It will just slow you down and you will struggle trying to swing the bat. The bat will look like it's swinging you instead of you swinging it. Use a bat that you can control easily. Most young children are not physically strong enough to swing the larger bats.

Little league players, if unable to choose between one length of bat and another, should always use the smaller of the two. You want to have a bat that will be light enough and short enough so that when your brain and body figure out the path by which you want the bat to hit the ball, it will get there in the quickest way possible, without having to drag the bat to the baseball.

I've played with a couple of professional baseball players who used exceedingly small bats. The best and most consistent hitter I ever saw in my career was Al Oliver. I was fortunate enough to play with him in Toronto during my last season in the majors. Al used a 33-inch bat and his lifetime average of over .300 justified its effectiveness. Bake McBride of the St. Louis Cardinals used a 32-inch bat and won a batting title with it. It is not how big and long a bat is, it is how effectively you use it.

I also do not believe in the theory of choking up on a bat. If the need to choke up on the bat is there, please use a smaller bat so that the hands are flush against the knob of the bat. It is very difficult to get a good grip on a bat if you have to choke up on it. Also, if you choke up, there is no knob on the bat that you can rest your bottom hand on to prevent slippage. I've seen little rubber inserts that go right above the knob of the bat. You can rest your hands on the insert, and it gives you the feel of choking up while still having something to rest your hands on. That is acceptable. You can find these at your local sporting goods store.

It is difficult to develop a guideline that would match a child's age with the size of bat he should use because children often vary in size and strength. Little Leaguers up to the age of 12 should not use anything larger than a 31-inch bat. During our 1993 championship season, we had a couple of 32-inch bats given to us, and our 12-year-olds had a little success with them and that was it. You could not tell them that they would be more successful if they used a smaller bat because the few hits they made sent their confidence level sky high. It was too late, because I did not want to do anything to hurt their confidence in the 32-inch bat. At that point in

JEFF BURROUGHS' INSTRUCTIONAL GUIDE

the playoffs, I did not care if they used a totem pole to get a hit if they believed it would work.

The general rule, though, is the smaller the better.

The Grip

The grip of a baseball bat is probably a little bit over-engineered. In order to be a good hitter, there are a few musts in the grip, but generally if it does not feel comfortable to you, it probably will not work. You will automatically change your own grip until you find one that is comfortable.

Jack Nicklaus used to describe how to grip a golf club by letting his hands dangle in front of him and gently slipping the golf club into them. He was trying to prove the point that the most functional and comfortable grip is the natural one. That's also a reasonable way to figure out your grip on the bat. One common theme that runs through all the teachings of hitting is balance and comfort. They also apply to the grip. It must feel comfortable to you, to the point where you do not have to think or worry about it.

In a lot of instructional books and videos, the instructors talk about the concept of having the knuckles on one hand line up with the knuckles on the other hand. Try it, it does not work. If you were to swing with your hands placed like that, I believe your baseball career would be over before it started. It is not comfortable.

When I grip a bat, the knuckles of my top hand are pointed at the middle joints of my bottom hand. This is comfortable to me, but it might not be to you. Find the position that is comfortable to you.

The bat should be held so that the palms of your hands meet the tips of your fingers. The fingers should wrap all the way around the handle of the bat. For young kids, this is sometimes difficult because of the small size

◆

6

of their hands, but they should try to wrap their hands around the bat as much as possible while remaining comfortable. The top hand should cradle the bat. The palm should be pointed up to the sky, taking some of the weight off your hands.

The bat should rest in the fingers because there is much greater feel and control of the bat when it is in your fingers instead of your palms.

The right and left hands should be touching each other on the bat. You are trying to get your hands to work together as much as possible. This is best accomplished by keeping them together, acting as one unit.

Ty Cobb, the great Detroit Tiger Hall of Famer, used an unorthodox batting grip and did fairly well with it. He held his hands eight inches apart on the bat. I could never figure out how that method worked for him, but a lifetime average of .367 meant it felt comfortable, to say the least.

Here, in order, are six steps to a good sound basic swing:

1. Become relaxed and comfortable.

2. Get in the set position.

3. Attack position.

4. The stride and weight shift.

5. Swing.

6. Follow-through.

1. Relaxed and Comfortable

Before we get into our stance we have to become relaxed and comfortable in the batter's box. We are trying to eliminate any tension that may develop. You cannot swing well with any amount of tension at all. You have to be relaxed, comfortable and balanced and remain that way until the pitcher begins his windup. You cannot get into your stance and hold it steady for a very long time. The longer you rigidly hold that stance, the more tension will come into your stance.

The first step is to make sure you have a good secure area in which your back foot can be comfortable. Try not to rest your foot in any holes or bumps. Try to find some flat ground to rest your back foot on so you can push off and pivot on it without slipping. Make sure that your back foot is close enough to home plate so that after striding (step 4) you can easily cover the outside corner of home plate.

Spread your feet out a little farther than shoulder width so you can develop a good, solid foundation. The feet have to spread out at least this wide to maintain proper balance. The closer your feet get to each other, the easier it is for you to lose your balance somewhere in the swing.

While you are in the box waiting for the pitcher to begin his windup, you can relax your body. Try rocking slightly back and forth while holding the bat down in front of you. Even alternately picking up your feet will help relieve any tension that can accumulate. Move the bat back and forth in front of you in conjunction with your body. This will help relieve the tension and stress that can build up in your hands and arms if you just stand there motionless awaiting the pitch.

This is similar to a golfer's waggle right before he begins his swing. The waggle is done to relieve tension in the golfer's body. Our rock serves the same purpose.

2. The Stance and the Set Position

The stance is truly an individualistic effort. If you watch the professionals on television, you will realize that there really is not one particular stance that they all use. Everyone is different.

Ballplayers use a stance that is comfortable and balanced to them. This has been successful for them and it is the way they make a living. All ballplayers experiment with different batting stances until they find one that works for them. For the purpose of instructing beginning ballplayers, the stance that I am promoting is the easiest, most workable stance of them all.

There are three basic stances: Open, closed or square.

In an open stance, your front leg and hip are opened towards either first or third base depending upon whether you are lefthanded or righthanded.

In a closed stance your front leg and hip are closer to home plate than your back leg and hip. This stance prevents you from opening your hips too soon after the ball is thrown and thereby pulling off the ball. What usually happens with overcompensating for a problem, even though you try and prevent it from happening, you end up opening up too much anyway.

In a square stance, your front shoulder, hip and knee are square to the pitcher. This is the stance I prefer to teach. It is the one that is by far the most workable.

Your weight should be on the balls of your feet. To ensure that your weight is forward, bend the body at the waist first, then the knees and then try to touch the ground in front of you. Your weight will automatically go to the balls of your feet.

Your hands should be above your shoulders or at the top of the strike zone with the bat at a 45° to 90° angle. They have to be in this position in order to make solid contact with the high strike. You cannot make solid contact if you have to raise your hands and bat upward to hit the ball. You can drop your hands to hit the ball lower than where your hands and bat have originated but not vice versa. You have to start your swing with your hands even with or higher than the plane of the ball. If you try to hit a ball higher than where your hands originate, the

◆

best you could do would be a high pop fly or foul ball, with the majority of those swings missing the ball entirely.

Do not wrap the bat around your head. It will slow down the reaction time when you decide to bring the bat to the ball.

The back elbow should be pointed down, not up, and fairly close to your body.

Weight should be shifted to the back side with approximately 60% on your back leg and 40% on the front.

The head should be turned and facing the pitcher. It would be nice if you had your eyes open too.

Now that you are relaxed and comfortable in the batter's box awaiting the pitch, you are in the set position. You must be in the set position when the pitcher begins his windup. Too often I see hitters still moving and fidgeting around when the pitcher begins his windup. This makes it very difficult to focus and concentrate on the task ahead. More often than not, when this happens the hitter is either late in his swing or off balance when the swing begins. In other words, get set before the pitcher begins his windup.

The body is now relaxed, comfortable and alert.

3. Attack Position

When the pitcher is at the top of his windup and he begins to turn his body to get ready to throw the pitch, you should prepare to begin your swing with one of the most critical elements of batting: getting the body in the attack position.

Get into the attack position when the pitcher turns his body to deliver the ball to home plate. The hitter should simultaneously shift his weight until it is against his back leg and turn his shoulder, hips and front leg inward to develop torque. The hands and weight should move slightly back with the shoulder

◆

turn to maximize power. The weight should be approximately 80% on the back leg. The body is now in a position to swing immediately once the path of the ball has been established.

I have seen a lot of young hitters who never get into the attack position before the pitch has been thrown. They are never ready at the moment they should stride and swing. This is the major reason why most young hitters swing late. It's crucial to be in the attack position BEFORE the pitch is delivered to the plate, not after.

If you ever want to drive the ball hard with any authority you have to get into the attack position.

Why is the attack position so important? You must get your body in a position where it has maximum power and quickness. Let me try to explain by example. Everybody is familiar with a shotputter, I hope. The object of a shotputter is to throw a heavy round ball as far as he can. What does that shotputter do before he throws that ball? His feet are balanced and he twists his body, or coils and shifts his weight to the backside. He is trying to develop as much torque as he can in order to throw the ball with as much force as he possibly can. This movement is only natural when you are trying to power the ball as far as possible. That position the shotputter is in before he throws the ball is his attack position.

Another illustration: Try to imagine you are going out to chop down a tree with an axe. What would you do? Would you just take the axe and gently tap the tree? This would take forever to do the job. What you would naturally do before you begin to hit the tree is to get into the attack position. You would take the axe back, shift your weight back and twist your body so you could deliver a tremendous impact toward that tree. This is exactly what a young hitter should do in the batter's box. Get in that maximum power attack position before the pitch is on the way.

◆

4. The Stride and Weight Shift

What we try to teach is to get in the attack position and stride after the ball leaves the pitcher's hand. "Stride and glide, stride and glide, make sure the ball is released before you stride" is a popular refrain we use with the kids to get that point across.

If you do stride too early, or before the ball has been thrown, you will be lunging and end up way out in front of the ball. If the pitcher throws you any off-speed pitches when you are in this position, it will be almost impossible for you to hit it with any authority.

If you begin your stride too late or after the ball has been thrown, your swing will be late and you will not be able to get the bat properly extended.

A well-timed stride is one that has to be worked on constantly until you feel comfortable with it.

When the ball is thrown, make an aggressive step towards the pitcher with the front foot and knee closed or pointed at home plate (turned in). Having the foot and knee closed will prevent you from opening up too soon or what is commonly called "bailing out." You cannot bail out with the front foot and knee closed.

Your stride should be a sensible one. A six-inch to 12-inch stride is optimal. If you stride too far, guess what? You will get off BALANCE. There is that word again. If you do not stride enough you cannot maximize your power.

When you are striding, your torso is still twisted and your hands are still in the attack position. This is another must. Your hands must remain back when striding. They cannot go forward with your stride. This is a very common bad habit to get into. If your hands go forward, the whole machinery will break down. You will lose all power and the ability to swing the bat correctly at the ball. You will be fooled on any type of off-speed pitch, and you will not be able to open your hips correctly. Plus, you will lose your balance. It is impossible to take a good swing at the ball if you get your hands in this position. I cannot over emphasize this fact.

As the front foot lands make sure that the front toe and knee open up to a 45° angle. This will make it easier for your hip, shoulder and weight transfer to proceed smoothly. Make sure you do not open up more than 45° or you will start to bail out and you will again lose your balance.

The front foot should land on the ball of that foot, not the heel, to prevent your body, especially your hips, from locking up. Landing this way will give you the ability to react to the ball more easily.

A proper weight shift is crucial if you are going to hit the ball with any power. You are trying to get your weight back to start with. Once the ball is located, you are able to throw all your weight and power into the ball through your stride, to hit it as hard as you can. The only way to do this properly is to start with approximately 75% of your weight on your back leg. The weight must go back before it can go forward to hit the ball powerfully.

5. The Swing

The ball is now on its way to home plate, we have completed the stride, our hands are still back in the attack position, our weight is beginning to shift to our front leg and the swing begins. Let's hope at this point our mechanics are in place so we can be assured of making a good swing. All parts of a baseball swing are interrelated. If one part is wrong, the whole swing will probably break down and make it more difficult to hit the ball with any authority. In theory, we are striving for the perfect swing every time; in reality, if you can take two or three perfect swings a game, you are doing well. What we are trying to achieve is to cut down on the amount of bad swings we take.

◆

The weight shift is beginning, the hands are still held back at the top of the strike zone, the hips and shoulder are cocked. Your head is still. You are now ready to make a quick, explosive and aggressive movement towards the baseball.

Your hands must be in place, level with the top end of the strike zone with the bat at a 45° to 90° angle. I believe that it is imperative to begin your swing with your hands in this position so you can attack the ball without any unnecessary delays.

Begin the actual swing of the bat by pulling down level with your lead arm: if you are right-handed this is your left arm, and if you are left-handed it is your right arm. The bottom of our lead arm's hand should drive right at the ball. This movement will ensure that you are making a good level pass at the ball.

Too many times the back side of a hitter's body will take over the baseball swing at this point and create both an improper weight shift and an uppercut swing. This is natural because most right-handed hitters are right-handed in everything they do, from eating, writing, lifting an object, shooting a basketball, etc. You simply exercise that arm or side of your body a lot more than you do your other one, and subsequently it gets a lot stronger. When one arm gets a lot stronger than the other, you will find that it will try and take control or dominate your swing. You have to work very hard to compensate for this problem and teach your front arm to lead your baseball swing.

Using this logic about dominant and subordinate arms in your baseball swing would mean that the best of both worlds would be throwing right-handed and batting left-handed. In this case, your dominant arm and side would be your lead arm. This would be the arm that would have the strength to drive the front arm directly to the baseball with the least amount of resistance, thereby making it easier to make solid contact with the ball.

◆

If you look at some of the greatest hitters in the game, a lot of them have had a right-handed throw and left-handed hit, or left-handed throw and right-handed hit combination. This theory is supported by some of the greatest hitters the game has ever seen: Stan Musial, Ted Williams, Pete Rose, George Brett, Rod Carew, Yogi Berra, Don Mincher (just kidding, Don, if you happen to read this), etc. Even some of the left-handed throw, left-handed hitters that have reached Hall of Fame status (Babe Ruth, Lou Gehrig) did everything but throw and hit a baseball right-handed which strengthened the front side of their bodies for a baseball swing.

Pulling down the front arm into the ball will also guarantee a level swing if your hands are in the right position to start with, and it will prevent you from dropping your hands before you swing.

We have all been told over the years how important it is to swing level, but how many people really understand why this is so crucial?

Let me illustrate. Visualize one object, the ball, coming at you from one direction and another object, the bat, coming from another direction. If you are swinging the ball either up through the strike zone or down through the strike zone (this hardly ever happens), the spot where the two objects can meet is so small and the timing has to be so perfect that it makes it very difficult for anyone to make solid contact with the two objects.

A level swing will permit you to hit a lot of ground balls and line drives, which is what you are striving for. A ground ball has to fielded, thrown accurately and caught to prevent you from reaching base. A fly ball only has to be caught. You then have a three times better chance of reaching base safely via a ground ball than a fly ball. A level swing will also enable you to hit the ball the other way, (right field if you are a right-hander, left field if you are a left-hander). A person with an "uppercut swing" cannot hit the ball the opposite way with any authority. It is just not possible.

Try to think about hitting through the baseball. You do not swing at the baseball, you try to hit through it. This will help with your extension.

At this point, your weight has begun to shift from your back leg forward.

Hitting Against a Stiff Front Leg

You have now shifted your weight forward and swung the bat aggressively through the strike zone. Your weight is now 75% on your stiff front leg. You must swing against a stiff front leg to again achieve maximum impact.

To illustrate this point. Imagine a car speeding along at 50 miles per hour. What do you think would make a greater impact: driving into a brick wall or driving head-on into a haystack? I think a greater impact would be made into the wall that has no give to it than into a soft haystack with a lot of give. The same holds true in the baseball swing; we are striving for maximum impact. A collision of one object into another. We want to throw as much of our weight as we possibly can into the ball. The way to do that is to start with our weight back, shift it and swing against a stiff front leg with full arm extension.

Back Leg

The back leg, and especially the back foot, is another important cog in the making of a sound baseball swing. Once the swing has begun, the back foot pivots or rotates on the ball or toes of the foot and drives off, with the weight transferring to the front leg. This is another must and it is overlooked quite frequently. If this movement does not take place, you cannot make a good fundamental swing.

◆

The pivoting of the back foot allows the hips to open up naturally. I do not teach much hip theory in my coaching because if everything else is done properly and the back toe pivots, the tips will automatically clear out, making it possible for the bat to come swiftly through the strike zone. I am not downgrading the importance of the hips in the swing. I just believe your hips will function the correct way if you adhere to the proper fundamentals.

If the back foot does not pivot, it will make it absolutely impossible for the hips to open, thus preventing any chance at a good swing. This is what is referred to as blocking out the hips.

Head

Throughout this entire process, the head must remain still. OK, simple enough! Easier said than done, however. Even at the professional level, one of the most common mistakes in the baseball swing is pulling your head off the ball. The major reason this happens is trying to hit the ball too hard or attempting to pull the baseball. You will have to continually remind the kids about staying on the ball.

During the swing a lot of things can and do go wrong, but contact can still be made. Often, you can still put the ball into play with a faulty swing. I guarantee you, however, that you will never have any success at all as a hitter if you do not look at and concentrate on the baseball. This is the number one must.

In golf the ball does not move, but the motions of a golf swing and a baseball swing are very similar (the launch position, the weight transfer, etc.). When Jack Nicklaus first began playing golf, his teacher used to hold his head as still as he could with both hands while the future golf star would hit hundreds of balls. He was trying to teach Jack the importance of keeping his head still. It obviously must have worked.

◆

In baseball, it is just as true. You cannot hit the ball without focusing on the object you are trying to hit. If the head moves during the swing, the odds are stacked against you hitting the ball hard. Your body must rotate around your head. Your success as a hitter will coincide with how still and steady you can keep your head.

When you miss the ball completely keep your head still and focused out in front of home plate. When a pitch is made and you decide not to swing at it, try to get into a habit of following the ball back into the catcher's glove. This is another method of teaching your body to concentrate on the ball at all times.

6. Follow-through

Follow through with the bat high or at shoulder height with your back toe and hips rotating so when the swing is completed your belly button is facing the pitcher.

Be sure to hang onto the bat with both hands after contact. I know a lot has been written and taught about letting go of the top hand, but I do not think it works well with young kids, especially ones that are just beginning. If you are taught to hold onto the bat with both hands it makes it a lot easier for your hips and shoulders to open up.

If at the end of your follow-through you are still holding the bat with both hands, your hips and shoulders will automatically pivot or open up to free the rest of your body to make a good swing at the ball.

If you let go of the bat with the top hand, a lot of times the pivot of the hips and shoulder do not take place and then a correct fundamental baseball swing cannot be made.

Mental Aspects of Hitting

Preparation

While you are on deck awaiting your time at bat, go through a set routine by which you will get some benefit from being on deck instead of just looking around to see if your girlfriend is watching. I recommend going through a series of movements just as you would if you were in the batter's box. Take your batting stance and get balanced and comfortable. Put some movement into your stance as you await the make-believe pitcher's windup. Get relaxed and comfortable, get set, get back into the attack position, stride, shift your weight and pivot on the ball of your back foot just like you would in the batter's box. Follow through. Try to make a perfect fundamental swing.

You have to keep repeating and repeating this swing thousands of times until your muscles can memorize these movements so they will know what is expected of them without you consciously doing it.

It is like learning to play the piano. You have to keep practicing specific movements until your mind can memorize them accurately. Do it over and over again until you can make a sound baseball swing without having to think about it.

Before you get in the box, study the pitcher to see how hard he is throwing and where he is throwing: overhand, sidearm, etc. Does he throw many curveballs? Is he wild? Prepare yourself for the at-bat.

Once you are in the batter's box, think about driving the ball right back at the pitcher. Be aware of the outside part of the plate. The stride should always take place away at the outside of the plate rather than inside or over the middle of the plate. If the pitch is on the outside

◆
19

part of the plate your body will be ready for it and you should try to hit the pitch the other way, or to right field if you are a right-hander and to left field if you're a left-hander. If this pitch is down the middle, drive it up the middle, and if the pitch is on the inside of the plate, pull it to left field or to right field if you are left-handed.

Looking away for the pitch lets you react to the ball because your weight is still going toward the pitcher. If the ball is thrown down the middle or on the inside part of the plate you can adjust accordingly. You cannot look for a pitch on the inside part of the plate to hit and adjust to the pitch down the middle or on the outside part of the plate. You can, however, look away and react to the ball in.

These are obviously general parameters. When I say look away, I do not mean that you have to be ready to hit the perfect pitch on the outside corner. This is what I call "No Man's Land." No one should be able to or expect to hit a ball right on the corner. This is a pitcher's pitch, and if he can throw a ball there he deserves credit for it. Ted Williams, my first manager, said that if every pitch could be thrown on the outside corner, even he would not have hit over .200 in his career. I do not want you to look for a ball that will come right down the middle either. Start by looking for the pitch to come down the outside part of the plate, not the outside corner, and react accordingly.

Try to utilize the entire playing field. It only makes sense to try to hit the ball where it is pitched.

Harmon Killebrew was a Hall-of-Famer with tremendous power. He was a dead pull hitter. This means that as a right-handed hitter he almost never hit the ball to the right side of second base. The other team knew this so they would play all of their players with the exception of the first baseman and right fielder on the left side of the bag. With that many people playing on the left side, there was a great reduction in the area where a ball can drop in without getting caught. This really hurt his batting average, but he was more concerned with home runs than his batting average, anyway.

◆

It just makes more sense to use the whole field. It will give you a greater chance of hitting the ball to a spot where there are no fielders, and it will give you a better chance for success.

Think about hitting the ball on a line or ground ball right back toward the pitcher and then react accordingly to where the actual pitch is. Have an idea when you get to the batter's box. Do not just wander up there aimlessly.

Never, never try to lift the ball in the air for a home run. Home runs come by accidents at any level. Most home runs are hit when you are not trying for them.

When I was playing, 80% of my home runs came after two strikes when I was just trying to make contact. A correct fundamentally sound baseball swing with full extension will result in hitting the ball farther and harder than you ever thought possible. The harder you try and hit the ball, the more tension will develop in your body. When tension does develop, your swing breaks down and you actually swing slower, not faster, through the strike zone.

Swing and think aggressively. Swing the bat hard when you are up at home plate. Being aggressive can compensate for a lot of other shortcomings. Condition yourself to believe that if a ball is thrown in the strike zone, you are going to make a good pass at it. The only way you are going to get some hits is to swing the bat.

Do not be afraid of failing. Everybody strikes out. Give it your best shot, be happy that you tried as hard as you did and prepare for the next at-bat.

The next step is practice. This is a must. You can never expect to be a good hitter without practice and lots of it.

Ted Williams, the greatest hitter ever, actually believed that the reason he was such a terrific hitter was not that he was so incredibly talented, but because he worked at it so hard. That might be stretching it somewhat, because you do have to have some talent to begin with to be the kind of hitter he was, but the principle is true. If you practice and practice and practice hitting the baseball the right way, you will get the most out of your talent. When you become successful at it, you will derive a lot of pleasure out of knowing you gave it your best shot.

There is no shortcut. You will become proficient at hitting a baseball only equal to the desire and hard work you put into it.

I get a lot of calls from parents asking me to help them teach their children how to hit. They explain that their children have been taught my methods, but they do not understand why their children are having so much trouble hitting the ball. I ask the parents how much time the children have spent practicing what I have taught them. Usually the reply is "not much."

The parents truly believe that one or two days of them explaining the fundamentals in this book will instantly make their children into great hitters. It does not work that way. True, you have to have a good foundation and you have to know the correct way to hit, but without a lot of time spent practicing these proven fundamentals, you will not become a good hitter.

So my advice to you is, teach the fundamentals found in this book and practice them correctly. They work, there is no question about it.

Bunting

Bunting is a truly forgotten art in baseball. A correct and well-placed bunt can completely alter the tone of a ballgame. It is also rarely taught correctly or practiced enough.

The Grip

Slide your top hand to about midpoint on the bat so that you can control the bat easily with your top hand even if you let go of the bat with your bottom hand. Lightly pinch the bat with your thumb and index finger, being careful to keep all fingers on the back of the bat. This will keep your fingers out of the way and prevent the ball from crushing your fingers on the bat.

The barrel of the bat should be a little higher than the knob of the bat.

The Stance

Get up in the box, closer to the pitcher than normal. This will allow for a better angle to bunt the ball in fair territory.

When the pitcher begins the windup, pivot on your back foot until you are facing the pitcher and keep your weight evenly balanced. Hold the bat out in front of you over the plate making sure that you can cover the outside part of the plate. Keep your bat away from your body. This will make it a lot easier for you to see the ball make contact with the bat. Do not hold the bat too close to your body because you will end up losing sight of the ball before contact is made.

Hold the bat up at the top end of the strike zone. Just like hitting a baseball, the bat must be held in this position to bunt the ball correctly. You can always lower the bat to bunt the ball fair. You cannot and should not ever raise the bat to bunt the ball. A good rule: Never attempt to bunt the ball higher than where you start the bat from. Trying to raise the bat to bunt the ball will usually end up in missing the ball or worse, popping it up to a fielder.

When the pitch is thrown, position the bat over the top end of the ball's path and let the ball hit the bat. Do not try and hit the ball when bunting, just get the bat in the path of the ball. Try to cushion the ball, or deaden it, by pulling back on the bat at the moment of contact.

To bunt the ball at the pitcher, hold the barrel and handle of the bat equidistant from your body.

◆

To bunt the ball to first base, if you are a right-handed batter, pull the barrel of the bat closer to your body in order to develop the correct angle so the ball will carom off the bat toward first base.

To bunt the ball toward third base, pull the handle of the bat in towards your body with the barrel of the bat out in front of home plate creating the proper angle.

Do not lower or raise either the barrel or handle end of the bat when attempting to bunt the baseball. The angle of the bat should remain level throughout the attempted bunt.

Drag Bunt

In drag bunting, or bunting for a base hit, you are trying to catch the defense sleeping, so be careful not to give away what you are trying to do to the other team until the last possible moment.

Right-handed Hitter

When the pitcher is about ready to release the ball, step back with your back foot to get into position to run as soon as contact is made. Slide your top hand up on the bat and pull the handle of the bat into your body creating an angle that will bunt the ball to third base.

Left-handed Hitter

Execute the bunt to third the same way as you would make a sacrifice bunt except you wait a little longer to commit yourself to the play.

Right-handed Push Bunt

On a push bunt, you are trying to push the ball past the pitcher towards the second baseman. This is an especially good play in a sacrifice situation with the second baseman covering first base. If you can manage to get the ball by the pitcher and the first baseman charging towards second base, you will have a sure base hit because there is nobody left to field the ball (the second baseman is covering first).

Bunt the ball just like you would bunt it towards first, but instead of bunting it softly, push the bat at the ball with the correct angle towards second base.

Bunting is a potent offensive weapon if used correctly. It must be practiced as much as possible to become proficient. Schedule some practice time during every practice to work on the fundamentals of bunting.

Baserunning

In my first year of coaching I was in the first base coaching box giving my five-year-old tee-ball player instructions on what to do after hitting the ball. I told him to wait and make sure the ball is hit in the air, not to run until it hits the ground, to run and slide into second if a ground ball is hit to the infielders and to run to third if the ball is hit past the infielders to the outfield. Our hitter then proceeded to hit a line drive to right field and, following directions perfectly, ran to third base. Only he forgot to go by way of second. The pitcher had to jump to get out of his way or he would have run the pitcher over on his way to third base.

When the laughter subsided after that play, I realized that I took for granted that the child would know

◆

how to run the bases. We had never practiced baserunning. It was not the kid's fault, it was the coach's. The kid was only following directions. Needless to say, at our next practice baserunning was at the top of our list.

Baserunning is often an overlooked aspect of coaching youth baseball. It's also one that is difficult to cover in a book because of the myriad of possible baserunning situations. The best and easiest way to practice and teach baserunning is covered in Chapter 4, "Practice." Basically it comes down to practicing in game situations at every coaching session what might happen to your baserunners. Experience is the best teacher of all.

I will try to cover the basics and the most common mistakes of baserunning in this section. I will not cover in any detail anything concerning leading off. I have purposely omitted any mention of pick-offs and holding a runner on the bases in my pitching section because I do not believe that at this age a child should be playing baseball with lead-offs. It makes trying to learn a difficult game even more difficult, especially for children who are just starting out. I am in complete agreement with the Little League philosophy of no lead-offs. You have enough fundamental baseball to teach to the young children, some of whom have never played before, without having to spend half your practice time going over leading off.

I have seen numerous games in other leagues in which leading off is permitted in this age bracket. As a result, what you see is basically more of a track meet than a baseball game. Over the course of such a game there will be perhaps thirty stolen bases and maybe one person thrown at while attempting to steal. To me this is not baseball. I applaud the other leagues for providing the children a place and an opportunity to play, but I just wish they would stick to the basic fundamentals and abandon their lead-off rule. They'll have plenty of time to learn the art of leading off when they get older. Keep it simple, teach only the fundamentals and the kids will learn more and have more fun.

◆

Running to First Base After the Ball Has Been Struck

After the ball has been hit on the ground, run down inside the baseline to first base and try to land on the top of the bag. Do not try to land on the edge of the bag because of the possibility of injury. During my career I had the misfortune of landing on the edge of the bag with my heel one time, and I guarantee you it hurt. I could not run without pain for about two weeks. So make sure you land on top of the bag.

Run *through* the bag. Try to accelerate all the way across the bag instead of timing yourself to slow down when you reach the base.

Hit to the Outfield

On a base hit to the outfield, as you approach first base, run in an arc about 10 feet outside the baseline before you get to the base so you will be better positioned to cut the angle on your path to second base. Tag the inside corner of the base with either foot. I say either foot because young kids will more often than not break stride to make sure the correct foot hits the bag, which only slows them down. It does not matter which foot hits the base as long as you do not break stride.

We tell all our players: As soon as you know the ball is going through the infield and it is a hit, do not assume that it's just going to be a single. Always think about trying for a double. Make a wide turn around first base thinking about trying for second without breaking stride or slowing down.

This will enable you to get a jump toward second base if one of the outfielders bobbles the ball or the ball is hit a little bit more between the outfielders than you thought. If the outfielder does come up with the ball cleanly, all you have to do is slow down and retreat back to first base. He is not going to throw you out at first base from the outfield position.

What usually happens on a base hit is that the hitter makes a small turn around first base and slows down. Then, if the outfielder misplays the ball, the baserunner tries to reaccelerate and run toward second. But the outfielder now has time to recover and throw the ball to second and put the runner out just because he lost those precious few seconds when he took for granted the outfielder was going to field the ball cleanly. Never take for granted that the defense will make the play. Be aggressive on the basepaths. This aggressive style of baserunning should be used on all the bases, not just first base. Always be alert for the chance to take that extra base.

Know How Many Outs There Are

Whenever you are on base, you should ask yourself after every pitch how many outs there are. If you aren't sure, ask the base coaches. *Always* know how many outs there are.

When there are less than two outs, be prepared to run when a ground ball is hit. Be sure not to wander too far off the base if a popup is hit to an infielder. When a fly ball is hit to the outfield, do not commit yourself to running or going more than halfway to the next base until the ball hits the ground.

With two outs, be prepared to run as soon as the ball is hit, whether the ball is hit in the air or on the ground.

If you are on first base when the ball is hit safely to right center or right field, start your run to second.

Before you begin to make your arc to turn on second, look up and find your third base coach. He will tell you whether or not to continue to third base by his hand motions. It is a lot simpler to look to your third base coach for guidance than to turn your body around to look and see where the ball is. It is very difficult to run full speed, tag the base and look behind you all at the same time.

If you are on first base and the ball is hit in front of you, proceed on your own judgment. When the ball is in front of you where you can see it, you can make your own decision because you can see what is happening without having to slow down and turn around.

Tagging Up On Fly Balls

In my nine years of coaching youth baseball, tagging up on fly balls is without a doubt the single most common baserunning mistake. It usually happens because the runner thinks the ball is not going to be caught. At the last moment, when it finally dawns on him that the ball is about to be caught, a mad scramble to get back to the base ensues, wasting precious seconds. By this time, the ball has been caught and is on its way back to the infield.

Have your runner on third get in the habit of tagging up on any fly balls or line drives hit to the outfield. Runners on first and second should proceed halfway to the next base and wait to see if the ball is caught or not.

Sliding into Second Base

If you are on first base and the ball is hit to an infielder, be sure to slide into second base. Do not even think of any other options; just slide into the bag. Too often, players are put out at second because they anticipated the play being made easily at second base and subsequently slowed down, when in fact they could probably have slid in safe.

Sliding

Sliding is a critical part of baserunning. If you remember the motto, "When in doubt, slide," when dealing with young players in a game, you will probably never have trouble with this aspect of baserunning. A baserunner should *never* get thrown out at a base without sliding. If there is any doubt whatsoever in the runner's mind as to whether to slide, he should give it a try.

There is nothing worse than your runner running to second on a potential force-out and taking for granted that the infielder will catch the ball and the put-out will be made there, only to see the infielder drop the ball and still have enough time to pick it up for the force-out because the runner gave up and did not slide into the base.

When a runner is on second base and a ball is hit to the outfield, the third base coach should tell the runner to slide no matter what when he gets to home plate. I would rather be safe than sorry. The on-deck hitter should rush over behind home plate directly in the runner's line of vision and let the runner know whether to slide or not by raising his hands to mean "stand up" or lowering his hands to mean "slide." There again, if there is any doubt as to whether to slide or not, SLIDE.

How to Slide

Every child slides a little differently. Some kids like to slide on their left sides and others feel more comfortable sliding on their right sides. It really makes no difference which side they slide on as long as it feels comfortable to them. At this age, there is no need to learn how to slide on both sides.

◆

Sliding is natural for kids this age. The most important thing to remember is to slide with your hands up in the air so you do not jam your hand against the ground during your slide. A good trick is to have the runners hold onto their batting gloves in each hand while beginning their slide. In order not to drop the batting gloves, the arms will naturally have to stay up off the ground during the slide.

Be extra careful when you slide not to jump directly on top of the base. This is probably the easiest way to get seriously hurt in baseball. The foot will hit and jam into the bag, with a broken foot or severely jammed ankle the result. You should hit the ground approximately five feet in front of the base and slide into it.

Pitching

The pitcher is without a doubt the most important player on the field. Everything revolves around the pitcher: balls, strikes, strikeouts, ground balls, fly balls, base hits, runs, etc.

The often-used phrase "good pitching always beats good hitting" is a true one. In professional baseball, you cannot name one world champion, or for that matter even a divisional champion, baseball team that did not have good pitching as its backbone. The chances of a hitting breakdown over the course of a season are much greater than the chances of a pitching breakdown simply because you basically start the same eight offensive players at the same time.

No person is more valuable than the pitcher. A team's hopes ride almost entirely upon a pitcher's back. When a pitcher is in a comfortable rhythm and throwing strikes, that team has a good chance to do well that day.

◆

When a pitcher looks uncomfortable and is having a hard time getting anybody out, it is obviously going to be a very long day.

The enjoyable part of teaching the fundamentals of pitching is that it is very coachable, so you can see the results of your efforts almost immediately.

Let us start with the baseball. After all, this is what you have to work with, and your opponent is trying to bash the living daylights out of it. The baseball weighs between five and five and one quarter ounces and has a circumference between nine and nine and one quarter inches. There are 108 stitches on the seam of each ball. How you handle this ball and how accurately you throw it will determine how much success and fun you will have.

Ball Dynamics

The trajectory of a baseball has three essential properties. I will list them in order of importance.

1. Location

The common belief is that the most important factor in achieving success on the pitching mound is velocity. But in fact, the most important criterion in purchasing a piece of real estate is also critical in pitching: LOCATION, LOCATION, LOCATION. It is impossible to defense a walk. It is of no value whatsoever to be able to throw a ball 300 miles an hour if you do not know where in the world it is going. If you can consistently throw the baseball where you want to, you will be a good pitcher. When I was playing professionally, Randy Jones of the San Diego Padres and Tommy John of the Los Angeles Dodgers were two pitchers who enjoyed tremendous success because they could throw the ball exactly where they wanted to. They could not throw hard enough to break a glass window, but their control was such that you could never quite hit the ball solidly enough to beat them consistently. There was a pitcher in the minor leagues on whom the Charlie Sheen character in the movie "Major League" was based—Steve Dalkowski—who has been credited with throwing the ball harder than anyone has ever thrown it, but he didn't spend one day in the majors because he could not throw strikes. Good location is the foundation of pitching success.

2. Movement

The importance of throwing a live ball ranks just below that of good location. Hitting a ball that moves on its way to home plate is like trying to hit a fly in the air. The sailing, sinking motion of the baseball will make it that much more difficult to hit the ball solidly with the bat. The end result will be a ground ball or a popup. A pitch that is thrown "straight," with no movement, is a lot easier to hit solidly. Good pitchers continually work on different grips to see which ones will make the ball move the best.

3. Velocity

The minor leagues in professional baseball are littered with what we call flamethrowers. Throwing the ball with "heat" is not of any benefit if you cannot throw strikes with it.

High velocity is a tremendous advantage if you can combine it with location. If you can't, it is of no value whatsoever.

◆

Keep in mind the three absolutes to pitching as we go through the fundamentals and keep going back to them in their order of importance: location, movement and velocity.

Equipment

Shoes

Do not underestimate the importance of good shoes. Last year during one of our Southern California championship all-star games, my son decided to try his new shoes that day. After a rather trying first inning, he had to go back to his old shoes that he had used all year because the new ones did not feel right and had thrown him off. If you buy new shoes, give yourself enough time to break them in before the regular season begins. Make sure the shoes fit comfortably and do not hurt either foot during the entire pitching exercise.

A toe plate that fits on the shoe that protrudes from the pitching rubber is a prudent idea to save your shoe from excessive wear and tear. The toe of that shoe has a tendency to drag as you push off from the mound, causing the toe to wear through prematurely. A toe plate, which can usually be bought at most sporting goods stores, will alleviate that problem.

Hat

Find a hat with a wide bill. You can conveniently hide vaseline or other preparations to put on the baseball to promote ball movement while the umpire is not looking. *Just kidding.*

Glove

Make sure you have a glove that you feel comfortable with. Remember, after you have delivered the ball to home plate you become another infielder ready to react to the ball wherever it is hit.

Be sure to buy a glove with a solid web. Avoid the H-web gloves because the batter can see through those and observe how you are gripping the ball. If he can tell how you are gripping the ball, he might be able to tell what kind of pitch you're throwing.

Preparation

Pitching can best be described as the attempt to throw strikes at different speeds in order to keep the hitter from hitting the ball solidly and with power.

The act of pitching is the sum act of coordinating the upper torso with the bottom torso to deliver a powerful controlled motion towards the batter. The upper body and the lower body have to act together in order to deliver a fluid motion to home plate. When one part of the body begins to act independently of the other, the chances of throwing the ball with power and accuracy diminish greatly.

The body must be able to repeat the exact same motion over and over again with no visible change.

The Baseball

Once you receive the baseball, step off the mound and rub some dirt into the baseball to remove the shine and slickness. It is difficult enough to throw a strike with a baseball that you can grip, let alone with one that is slick and hard to get a hold of.

The Rubber

The pitching rubber is a slab 24 inches long and 6 inches wide, 10 inches off the ground. You should find a spot on the mound where you feel comfortable. If you are right-handed, try to position yourself on the right side of the rubber so you can get a better angle on right-handed hitters. Remain in the same spot, even if you are facing a left-hander. We remain in the same spot no matter who is hitting because in pitching we are trying to repeat all the same movements over and over again. This also prevents you from tipping off the hitter, which might happen if you stood in one place for a curveball and another for a fast ball. Get used to doing the same thing over and over again.

Put your left foot approximately half a step in front of the right foot. Bend over at the waist and knees to ensure that your weight is forward.

This is your normal set-up position. It doesn't have to be exactly as I describe, though. Everybody is a little different. The important part is that you are set up looking in for your signs with your weight forward and comfortable.

Windup

The windup is a synchronization of all body parts to get the body ready to deliver the baseball. The windup prepares the body with rhythm and momentum to thrust itself towards home plate.

There is no absolute way to begin your windup; everyone is different. Some people are taller, heavier, wider than others. Each body style requires a different windup. Try to find your own particular style of windup that feels comfortable to you. Whatever style you choose, make sure that it is one you are able to repeat over and over.

Here at the top of the windup is when your right foot is parallel to the rubber in a position where you can push off from it.

Weight Shift

Yes, that's right. There is also a weight shift in pitching, just as there is one in hitting. Remember, any powerful motion forward has to be preceded by a move back. This is where you begin to generate some power. As you begin your windup, your weight will shift back towards your rear with the outside or lead foot stepping backwards behind the foot that is on the rubber. As your weight shifts back, your hands now start up. How high you go with your hands depends on what is comfortable for you. Keep practicing until you find a position that feels comfortable. I recommend going just over the top of your head with both hands still in the glove. When the glove is coming back down in front of your body, try to break your hands (or separate your throwing hand from your gloved hand) in front of your face. Again, this is not an absolute; practice until you find the spot where you feel relaxed.

Knee Lift

The knee lift is an integral part of the windup. It is used to balance the body and to initiate momentum and the coiling of the body to provide power to home plate.

◆

41

How high you lift your knee is an individual matter. There again, lift it only as high as is comfortable, so that you are balanced. A good test is to see how high you can go and then freeze your delivery. If you can maintain balance without falling one way or the other, you have probably got it right.

Once the knee is raised, your head should be perpendicular to the ground and over your knee. The shoulder, hip and knee will now rotate to the right until they are all lined up together and at least in a closed position relative to home plate. I say at least, because you want to make sure you rotate your body past home plate. Good rotation is where you generate a lot of your power. If you rotate too far, you might lose your balance. A lot of pitchers feel they have to rotate until the uniform numbers are facing home plate. That's fine if you can rotate that far and still coordinate all the rest of your body parts through the delivery. How far you rotate is something that should be practiced and practiced until you find your own style.

Getting into the Throwing Position

Now it is time to get to what is critically important—the throwing position. Like hitting and getting into the hitting position, the pitcher must get into the throwing position as soon as possible. That position involves getting the ball out of the glove at the break and getting it back behind your body as soon as possible. You cannot rush this movement. I have seen many times when a pitcher is more concerned with his windup or step or turn and misses one of the most important fundamentals of pitching— getting the ball out of his glove and back behind him. A lot of beginning pitchers tend to wait until it is too late to get the ball into the throwing position and end up off balance or rushing their delivery. Get the ball back as soon as you can while remaining balanced and comfortable.

Keeping Your Eyes on the Target

Young players just learning how to pitch should keep their eyes on the target at all times. Then when they get comfortable with their mechanics, they can look at the target as they begin the windup, take their eyes off it briefly, and pick up the target again when they begin the knee lift. This makes it easier to get young pitchers to make complete body turns.

Be sure to work with your catcher to give the target early, before the pitcher begins his windup. Sometimes the catcher will wait until the last minute to give the target, and this will confuse the pitcher who is about to throw the ball to home plate. A good tip is to make the catcher's knees the target. Practice trying to hit the catcher (but not literally) in the left or right knee.

The Stride

Your body is now in the throwing position. Your right side now dips slightly backwards. A right-hander gets a lot of power from the right side of his body. Just like the weight shift in hitting, in the stride the weight transfers from the back side to the front side. In this instance the left leg is absorbing the brunt of the force.

There is no absolute to how far you stride. I recommend striding as far as you can while still remaining comfortable and balanced. What *is* important is that you stride in the same spot every time.

In order to work on a correct stride, draw a line in the dirt directly from the middle of your back foot while it rests on the rubber to the center of home plate. When you stride, your lead foot should come down just outside of the line with your toe pointed right at home plate. Use this method whenever your players are practicing pitch-

◆

ing, and make sure they realize exactly where they are landing.

If the front foot lands too far outside this line, the body has opened up too much and the ball will usually go high and outside. If you stride too much to the inside of the line, you will be throwing what is called "across your body," and throwing this way usually leads to some type of arm problem, not to mention the inability to throw strikes. If you practice this drill and get the step down pat, your body will automatically be in the right position to throw the ball to home plate. Keep your body flexible.

As in most other areas of baseball fundamentals, the same basic theories apply. You have to be balanced and flexible. Probably one of the most important basics is to keep your back leg and especially your front leg bent. You have to land on your front leg when it is bent or flexible. If you do not do this you will be landing on a straight leg, and most times when you see a pitcher land on a straight leg the end result is not good. There has to be some give in your landing leg so you will be able to rotate your body toward home plate and use your legs to take the strain off your arm. Landing on a straight leg with no give will sooner or later result in arm problems because of the recoil effect that will occur when you throw against the stiff leg.

Landing on a bent or flexible front leg, on the other hand, will enable all parts of the body to work together. You will find yourself throwing harder, better and for longer periods of time.

The Glove Hand

Before the ball is actually delivered, one more thing absolutely has to happen. This is something that is often overlooked when coaches are attempting to teach young kids how to pitch—that is, what to do with the glove hand. In order for all the parts of the body to work with each other, the throwing arm must follow the same path as that of the glove hand. The glove hand leads the right side of the body toward home plate at the completion of the delivery.

Pull your left arm down in front of you at a 45° angle with the pocket of the glove facing you. The left arm should come to rest outside and below your left hip. Try to keep the arm from swinging back too far behind the body.

It is highly unlikely you will ever have a fluid throwing style that will yield strikes if you have a faulty glove arm. In order to consistently throw the ball where you want to, the glove arm has to lead or show the way for the pitching arm to throw the ball accurately. It is just too difficult to throw the ball at your target when one part of your body is going one way and the other parts are going another.

I cannot emphasize the importance of this movement enough. It is one part of the pitching fundamentals that is rarely taught, but without it, you almost certainly won't have a successful pitcher.

The Delivery

There are two essentials or absolutes in the delivery: the grip of the ball and where you hold your elbow.

Grip the baseball with your fingers on top of it, not to the side and obviously not underneath it. Young people have a hard time gripping it with two fingers on top because of the small size of their hands. Three fingers are okay if it is impossible to use two fingers on top. The problem you get into with the three-finger grip is that the directional finger is just one finger, the middle finger, while with the two-finger grip you are able to use both fingers as the directional fingers. It just makes sense

◆

that you will be able to control the baseball a lot better if you have two fingers trying to do the job instead of one.

Keep your fingers on top of the baseball. If your fingers are anywhere else, it will be very difficult to get the ball to go where you want it to. For example, the fastball is thrown with a flick of the fingers toward your target, and if your fingers are on the side of the ball, the ball may squirt out in any number of directions. The ball will not be able to rotate correctly on its path to home plate, either.

Keep your elbow above your shoulder and pull your arm down toward home plate at the same 45° angle at which your glove hand moved.

The body is designed to throw in a three-quarter style motion. It is actually impossible to throw the ball directly overhand and it is impractical to throw it sidearm. If the ball is thrown three-quarter, or from 10 o'clock on an imaginary clock, the arm is going directly at home plate for a great deal longer than it is when you throw it sidearm. If you make a mistake from a three-quarter motion, the ball will usually be only a bit high or low depending upon how long you held onto the ball. If the ball is thrown with a sidearm motion, it has to be released exactly at the right moment to be thrown accurately. If it is released too early it will be inside, if too late it will be outside, and you will still have to deal with throwing it at the correct level. Throwing three-quarter dramatically lowers the odds of throwing an inaccurate pitch.

Arc

The pitcher should try to throw a pitch with the widest arc possible while maintaining comfort and balance. The wider the arc, the greater the power. Imagine a professional golfer's swing: The bigger the arc, the farther the ball will go. Some players even buy a longer shaft for the golf club just so they are able to swing with a wider arc.

◆

Lee Trevino gave credit to his new, longer driver this year for adding 25 yards to his drives. The same rule applies to the pitcher. Keep the arm up as high as possible.

Follow-through

The follow-through is another of the musts. A correct follow-through will almost guarantee proper fundamentals and mechanics, and an improper one will almost guarantee faulty ones. Before the release of the ball, the pitcher should imagine throwing through the pitch rather than just releasing the ball. Drive your legs and backside and throw *through* the pitch. The entire windup should be accelerating from beginning to end with your throwing arm finishing outside and below your left knee, ensuring that your arm takes a 45° angle. If you do not finish outside your knee, you will not be accelerating correctly and you will be putting too much strain on your shoulder.

You should land slightly on the ball of your left foot. Do not land on your heel. If you land on your heel, it will cause your front leg to stiffen, and we now know that we want to land on a flexible front leg. *The right foot should land parallel to the other foot, not turned out, about shoulder width apart.*

Be balanced and comfortable, ready to catch or deflect any balls hit back at you.

Grips

Fastball

I don't really care how you grip the ball. Everyone is different. Just make sure that your fingers are on top of the ball no matter what type of grip you use. I will recommend the four-seam grip: two fingers on top with the third finger on the side of the ball and the index finger and thumb tucked underneath. Position your fingers on the spot where the seams make a horseshoe point to the right. This is the only grip in which all fingers and the thumb are on seams. Hold the ball lightly as much toward your fingertips as possible. Do not jam the ball back in the palm of your hand, since your fingers are what guide the direction of the ball.

Experiment with other grips. Find out how you have to hold the ball to make it sink, sail or move in other directions.

Curveball

I know I said I didn't recommend throwing a curveball at this age. The description of the curveball I am going to give you is not really a curveball; at least it is not thrown with the twisting and snapping of the normal curveball. We have used this one throughout our youth baseball seasons and find that it works just as well at this level as the sharp breaking one that hurts so many arms.

This is the only time I will suggest placing the fingers anywhere but on top of the ball.

Grip the baseball as you normally would for a four-seam fastball. Slide your first two fingers slightly to the right until your middle finger is resting against the bottom seam of the horseshoe. Move your index finger until it is up against your middle finger. Holding the ball this way, turn your whole hand and wrist to the right until your fingers are on the side of the ball. Throw this with the same 45° motion you normally would use for a fastball, but at about two-thirds of the fastball speed. Try not to slow your motion down too much so you don't tip the batter off about what is coming. Let the ball slip out between your thumb and index finger instead of being released by your first two fingers. Be careful not to twist your arm as you normally would with a curveball. What we are trying to achieve with this pitch is a change of pace with a slight break or arc to the ball. We are trying to create an illusion so that the batter does not know how hard the pitch is coming. You may have to practice this pitch a considerable amount before you're able to throw strikes with it, but do not give up.

Change-up

The change-up is just as effective a pitch as the curveball and will benefit your repertoire because it gives you another pitch to throw and another one for the batter to worry about.

There are any number of effective ways to hold the change-up. The important thing is to find one that is comfortable for you. One of the ways we teach it is to place the ball farther back in the palm of your hand instead of on your fingers. Slide the thumb farther up the right side of the ball than usual. Attempt to throw this pitch without slowing down your motion considerably, just as you're trying to do with the curveball. You are striving to throw all three pitches with basically the same throwing motion and exertion so the batter cannot tell what is coming. This pitch also has to be practiced quite a bit just to get comfortable with it. Don't stop practicing until you feel you can throw strikes with it.

Theory of Pitching

Too often during a game, I have seen youth baseball managers send a kid out to the pitcher's mound who has never even been on a mound before, let alone in an actual game. What chance do you think that kid has of performing well? Almost none. Even worse, he will come away with a bad feeling about pitching and probably will never want to try it again. Everything we do as coaches should be geared to providing as much coaching as humanly possible to prepare the kids. That way, when they go out on the field, they will know what to do, and most importantly, they'll have fun doing it.

The key to being successful at this level of play is just to practice until you are capable of throwing enough strikes to walk as few batters as possible. This only happens if you spend time practicing the fundamentals of pitching.

Never forget the old saying, "You cannot defense a walk."

Our 1993 Little League World Champion team walked 53 batters in 25 ballgames. Of all the statistics we compiled, I was most proud of that one. That averages out to a little over two walks per game. Consider that the World Champion Toronto Blue Jays averaged over three walks a game and you can understand how happy I am about that statistic.

Get ahead of the hitters. The most important pitch you throw is the first one. Concentrate on throwing a first pitch for a strike. Don't even worry about keeping the ball low in the strike zone. Throw a strike. More than 80% of bases on balls occur when the first pitch thrown is a ball. Even more astounding is the fact that in 76% of cases where the first batter of the inning walks, he scores.

I cannot stress enough how important it is to throw strikes. Even if you walk a batter who does not go on to score, you will end up throwing more pitches and working harder than you would if you threw strikes. Throw strikes and let the hitter hit the ball. The more strikes you throw, the more alert your fielders will be. The more batters you walk, the higher the probability that one of your outfielders will chase butterflies in the outfield instead of paying attention to the game.

◆

Do not make striking out every hitter your priority. Never lose sight of the fact that you have nine players on your side. If the hitter hits the ball fair, you have a chance to make an out. If you walk that hitter, there is no chance of a put-out.

I play a little game with my pitchers during practice and even carry it over into games sometimes. I get them to imagine changing the amount of balls it takes to walk. We practice three balls and three strikes. Try not to let the pitcher think he can throw three balls to the batter and get away with it. I keep reminding my pitchers that I don't want them to get to a three-ball count. Pretend a two-and-two count is actually a three-and-two count. Playing this little game with the kids will make them realize the importance of throwing strikes.

On the other side of the coin, if a pitcher can get ahead of the hitter 0-1 or 0-2, the hitter is now on the defensive. A study made during the 1992 major league season showed that all hitters hit an average of .191 with the count 0-2. That is incentive enough to concentrate on getting ahead of the hitter.

Once you get two strikes and no balls on the hitter, it is time to waste a pitch to see if your control is good enough to hit a corner. Our curveball is a good pitch to try to throw at 0-2 if you can throw it out of the strike zone. Try to land the curveball low around the catcher's shoe tops and preferably a little outside. Do not attempt to throw a 0-2 pitch for a strike. Make the hitter "fish" for the pitch. Remember, being ahead of the count makes the hitter wary of anything around the plate, so he's prone to swing at anything close.

I asked Gary Carter, the perennial all-star catcher with the Montreal Expos and New York Mets, what percentage of swinging third strikes are actually strikes. His reply was around 10%. That means that 90% of strikeouts recorded in the major leagues, by professionals who are paid to hit the ball, are out of the strike zone!

◆

Our teams in 1992 and 1993 used this theory to perfection. Half of the time if we even bounced the ball with a curveball on top of home plate with two strikes on the hitter, our opponents would swing at it. A very, very effective pitch.

To briefly summarize: To be a successful pitcher, *practice* the mechanics outlined in this chapter—and *practice* throwing strikes.

There is no bigger controversy in youth baseball than pitching. I have heard a thousand times the refrain, will pitching hurt an arm? Or especially, will curveballs hurt an arm? I am not a orthopedic doctor, nor do I pretend to be one, but I have talked to a lot of the leading team orthopedists in professional baseball and learned a lot from them about this problem. The consensus is, nobody really knows. Each situation is different. I will offer my opinion on this subject based on what I have learned and witnessed over the last six years with young pitchers.

Basically, there are three reasons why youngsters develop sore arms.

1. Some children do not have a throwing motion or style that is conducive to throwing a baseball. Time and time again I have seen a child on the mound pitching with such an unorthodox natural pitching style that a sore arm is inevitable. I believe that when you are born, you are given your own individual style of throwing a baseball one certain way and that way cannot ever be changed. You can change your fundamentals and pitching mechanics but you will never be able to change your individual style. It is not possible. It is like your fingerprints. There are no matching fingerprints anywhere; they are yours and yours only. The same holds true with your throwing style. A couple of years ago, two of the best players

on our team would complain of a sore arm
every time I pitched them in a game. Their
style could not take the strain of pitching.
Those individuals should never have been tried
as pitchers. There are plenty of other positions
available for the youngsters to learn and have
fun with.

2. Young pitchers do not learn the proper fundamentals. The human arm and shoulder were
not designed to throw an object with an overhand throwing motion. You have to *teach* your
body to do that. If you do not teach your body
the correct way to throw a baseball, the result
will be a sore arm. The correct fundamentals of
pitching must be taught so as to do everything
possible to relieve the strain from the shoulder.
The players who can incorporate these fundamentals should do the majority of the pitching.

3. There is too much emphasis on throwing curveballs. I have been asked this question a thousand times: "Do you think a young child should
throw a curveball?" Let me begin by saying
that I do not think a curveball, or what we
refer to as an off-speed pitch, when properly
thrown, is any more damaging to the pitcher's
shoulder than a fastball. Having said that and
after talking to several experienced medical
doctors about this subject, I would rather err
on the side of safety than take a chance of hurting a child's arm for life. I advise wholeheart-
edly against having a young child throw a
curveball.

What we teach to our youngsters is more of a
change-up than a curveball, and at this level it is just as
effective. The problem with teaching young pitchers to

◆

throw curveballs is that first and foremost their bodies have not grown enough to take all the strain the curveball will subject them to. Also, the coaches, for the most part, do not understand how a curveball should be thrown. If you do not have the proper fundamentals trying to throw a curveball, you will almost certainly develop a sore arm and in some cases never be able to throw correctly again. I have even been around a couple of young kids, and I mean 10- and 11-year-olds, who have actually had arm surgery because of throwing too many sliders or curves. That to me is very sad. There is plenty of time later on, when the kids' bodies mature, to learn to throw a curveball. Youth baseball is not the time.

Awaiting throw from the catcher on a steal. Feet have straddled the base. Knees are bent. Always be ready and alert for a bad throw. Anybody can catch a perfect throw.

Ball is caught and immediately put down in front of the bag so the runner will slide into it. The back of the glove is facing the incoming runner.

Wind-up. Hands over the head. Weight slightly on the back foot. Right foot is off the mound, which is a balk. Eyes on target.

Weight balanced on the right leg. Hip, knee and shoulder turn in for maximum torque. Chin over the knee.

The ball comes out of the glove. Shoulder, hips, and knee turn towards home plate. Left arm (glove hand) prepares to lead the way for the right arm. Eyes on target.

Right leg driving or pushing off the rubber. Arm back with thumb pointed down. Glove hand leading the way. Left foot striding and ideally landing in the same spot all the time. Eyes on target.

Weight on right leg has shifted forward. Left foot has landed with toes pointed directly toward home plate. Left knee is bent, not stiff and straight. Right arm has followed the same path as glove hand, finishing low and outside of left knee. Eyes on target. Perfect balance.

Weight has now completely transferred to a relaxed left knee. Right foot is coming forward so the pitcher can get ready for any balls hit back at him.

Fastball grip.

Curveball grip.

Change-up grip.

Knuckleball grip.

The force play at second. Ball is tossed underhand, just like a bowler, with the weight shifting forward. Be sure to show your teammate the ball so as not to surprise him. The player on second should be alert and ready for a bad throw.

Ground ball to the infielder's right. Pivot on the right foot and on your first step cross over with your left foot. Keep the glove down as low to the ground as possible. You can react up to a bad hop, but you can't go down to catch a bad hop.

Ground ball hit to the infielder's left. Pivot on left foot and on your first step cross over with the right foot. Keep the glove outstretched and as low as possible.

Fly ball outside. Throw should be caught with the thumb down, parallel to the ground.

Fly ball caught outside. Glove hand should be extended with the thumb pointed up.

Keep your eyes on the ball at all times.

On fly balls over your right shoulder, pivot on your right foot and cross over with your left foot, keeping your eyes on the ball at all times.

On fly balls over your left shoulder, pivot on your left foot and cross over with your right foot. Keep your eyes on the ball.

Infielders and outfielders catching ground balls. Start in the set position with hands on knees, weight slightly forward, knees bent and relaxed.

Pitch is made and weight goes forward with arms free and relaxed. Infielder and outfielder anticipate that the ball will be hit to them and know exactly what to do with it before it gets to them.

Ball is hit to the defensive player. Charge the ball under control. When the ball gets within 10 feet or so, bend over at the knees and waist and get the glove on the ground. Keep your legs spread apart as wide as you can while maintaining proper balance. Right foot is slightly behind left foot so you are able to turn and plant your right foot to get into position to throw. Ball is caught out in front of you, in line with the center of your body.

Simultaneously catch the ball and bring it into your chest to promote some give in your hands. This keeps the ball from bouncing out of the glove. Right foot should be slightly behind the left foot.

Place your body square to the target with a good grip on the ball.

Crow-hop (or take a step or two), then step toward your target and release the ball with a 3/4 delivery.

Relays: Ball should be fielded and thrown chest-high to the relay man. The relay man should raise his arms to provide a good target. Catch the ball and turn towards your glove hand. Square up to your target and throw the ball low.

The outfielder should catch the ball exactly as an infielder would. Keep the ball in front of you at all times.

Catch any ball thrown above your waist with the fingers of the glove pointed up or at a 45° angle.

If a ball is thrown below your waist, turn the glove around and catch the ball with the finger pointed down.

To tag second base on the double play, make sure your right foot is behind the base and your left foot is alongside the bag. Catch the ball first, then drag the top of your right foot across the bag.

On a bunt play, the second baseman should cover the first base bag with his left foot on the base to allow for greater lateral movement in case of a bad throw.

Give the pitcher a good target. Stay in a full squat with your weight on the balls of your feet. Keep your right hand behind your back to prevent its being hit by the ball. If the pitcher wants to try to hit the inside corner, slide over from this position until your chin is even with the outside part of the plate. Same thing for the outside corner.

On balls in the dirt, drop to stop the ball. Plug the hole between the legs with your glove. Keep your head down. Stay in front of the ball.

On the balls to the right, slide over and stay low.

Giving signs to the pitcher. Put your fingers against your inner right thigh to signal the pitcher. Make sure your knees aren't open too wide and your glove is below your left knee to prevent the third base coach from seeing your signs.

On balls to the left, slide over and try to keep the ball in front of you.

Pop-ups to the catcher. Take the mask off as soon as a pop-up is hit so you can see the ball in the air. Once you locate the ball, throw the mask in the opposite direction to keep it out of your way as you try to catch the ball.

On pop-ups, the catcher should always catch the ball with his back to the infield. The glove should be over his head. Notice how the mask is out of the way.

With runners on base, the catcher should be more on his toes and slightly out of the crouch to be ready for a steal.

Runners stealing. In this case the runner is stealing second. The catcher should square his body and step towards the target.

On balls hit to the outfield, always make a loop and touch the inside part of the bag. This enables you to get to second quickly.

Make a good turn and check to see whether the ball has been fielded cleanly. On all balls to the outfield, always be prepared to go for the extra base.

Slide with your knee bent underneath you. Keep your hands up in the air.

Do-or-Die play. When the winning run is on second, charge the ball and catch it outside your foot on the glove-hand side. Then square, step and throw.

Relax until the pitcher is ready to deliver the pitch. Try waggling the bat back and forth to relieve tension.

Before the pitcher begins the windup, get into the set position with your weight about 60% on your back leg. Hold the bat at the top of the strike zone at a 45° angle.

Before the ball leaves the pitcher's hand, rotate into the attack position.

Once the ball is thrown, stride toward the pitcher with your hands even with or above the level of the baseball.

Land on the ball of your front foot and begin your swing, pulling your lead arm level through the strike zone. Keep your eye on the ball.

Pivot and drive off the back foot on the follow-through. Finish with both hands on the bat.

Bunting: Turn your body to face the target, keeping the bat away from your body. Rotate the bat's barrel toward your stomach to angle the ball to third.

Pull the handle in towards your stomach to bunt the ball to third.

Fielding

During the '70s and '80s the dominating teams in professional baseball, the Oakland Athletics and Cincinnati Reds, were mainly known for their power hitting and the ability to score a lot of runs. They were also known in baseball circles as having tremendously talented defensive players.

Whether you are talking about the greatest soccer team, baseball team, basketball team or football team, if it was a championship team it had a great defensive ballclub. I cannot think of one championship team in any sport that did not have a gifted defensive squad. There is no substitute for catching and throwing the ball correctly. You do not want to give the opposition any more outs than you have to. If your defense makes too many errors, you may give your opponent four, five or six outs instead of three. When that happens, the other team will just have too many opportunities to score runs it would not have had if only you gave them only three outs.

Hitting a lot of home runs and scoring great numbers of runs is flashy and glamorous, but if you cannot

◆

hold the other side to the least amount of runs possible, you are going to have a lot of trouble winning ballgames.

Michael Jordan is best known for being the greatest basketball player ever because he is such an awesome offensive player. But anybody who really knows basketball also realizes what a tremendous defensive player he is. The Chicago Bulls won three NBA titles in a row because they were the best defensive team in the NBA.

The Washington Redskins and the Pittsburgh Steelers of the '70s won a couple of Super Bowls mainly because of their stalwart defensive play.

The German soccer team last won the World Cup not because they scored a lot of goals, but because the other teams had a very difficult time scoring any goals on them.

The point is if you are going to have a good baseball team, you have to learn how to play good defense.

The good news is that more than any other aspect of this particular sport, good defense can be taught. Pitching and hitting well usually deal with some individuals who have a lot of natural ability, but defense can be taught and enjoyed by anybody. It just takes a lot of practice.

On our world champion teams, we emphasized defense strongly throughout all of our practices. The work did indeed pay off. In 25 games in 1993, we made a total of 11 errors, a figure the 1993 New York Mets would be envious of. There is absolutely no doubt: If you want to have a successful team, you must really focus on defense and make as few errors as possible.

The Glove

I can't think of a better place to start talking about defense than a glove, and I mean a good glove. When I say a good glove, I mean a good, comfortable limber glove that fits the person using it. Do not outfit your child with a glove that you got as part of glove giveaway night at your favorite ballpark. Don't laugh, I've seen it happen. Parents want their children to become as proficient as they possibly can and yet they hand them useless tools that Ozzie Smith couldn't catch with. A glove is used to catch the ball, not just for the person to look good wearing it.

Find or buy your Little Leaguer a glove that fits comfortably. Do not buy a glove that he cannot control. A common mistake is purchasing a glove four sizes too big for him, the theory being that the bigger the glove is, the better chance of the ball going in. It does not work like that. Get a glove that fits comfortably and that he can control with his fingers. The idea is to close the fingers of the glove around the ball so the ball will not drop out. A glove that is too stiff makes that impossible.

To break in a brand new glove, get some neats-foot oil or some comparable product and massage it gently into the glove to loosen up the leather. Rub it into the entire glove, not just the pocket. Take a bat and pound it into the pocket to form a catching area. Take a softball and place it into the pocket of the glove. Manipulate the glove around the ball to where your hand would close naturally around the ball. Wrap some string around the glove to prevent the glove from opening up and hang the glove from a clothesline or something similar. After a few days, take it down and repeat the oiling process. If you do this a few times, the glove will begin to get softer. Now it is time to start using it to finish breaking it in. When you are done with your glove, always put a ball in it, to continue forming the pocket.

I do not recommend using a batting glove inside it as so many players do today. I believe it hurts the feel you want to get with your fingers inside the glove.

Infield Set Position

Before the pitcher begins the windup, you must get into the set position to prepare to field the ball.

◆

Spread your feet a little more than shoulder width apart and try to become as balanced as you can. The knees and the waist should be bent and relaxed and your weight should be slightly on the balls of your feet. Glove and hands should be on your knees.

Ready Position

When the pitcher begins the windup, shift your weight slightly forward and put your hands out in front of your body and as close to the ground as possible.

Anticipate the ball coming at you. Look around and size up the situation. How many outs are there, where are the runners, what is the score? What am I going to do with the ball if it is hit at me at a normal speed, what will I do if the ball is hit slowly? Is the runner slow, fast? Be aggressive; do not be afraid of making a mistake. I know that a lot of youngsters are secretly praying that the ball won't be hit at them because they are afraid of making a mistake. Everybody makes mistakes, though. Give it your best, and if you make a mistake, you have nothing to feel bad about. That is part of the game.

Fielding a Ground Ball

When the ball is struck and it starts coming at you, charge the ball under control. Then stop and get into position with your legs still apart and your body bent at the waist and knees to get as low as possible to the ground while maintaining good balance. Keep your legs spread as far apart as possible while maintaining balance. Try to catch the ball out in front of you where you can see it. Watch the ball go into your glove. Too many times a youngster's fundamentals are perfect except for the fact that he tries to catch the ball too far back between his legs and loses sight of the ball just long enough to miss it. Catch it out in front of your body and almost directly in line with your chin where you can see it. You are able to react to a bad hop a lot more easily with your glove out front. If you are positioned directly in front of a bad hop, the ball will hit you even if you aren't able to catch it. This will keep the ball from rolling into the outfield, preventing runners from advancing.

Keep your glove on the ground when you are ready to catch the ball. Never let a ball go under your glove. If you miss the ball, the ball should go over the glove, never under it. If the glove is on the ground when the ball takes a bad hop, it is a lot easier to raise the glove up to catch the bad hop than it is to go down to get it. In other words, it is a lot easier for your body to adjust upwards than it is to go down.

If you are right-handed, the right foot should be slightly in back of your left foot. This will allow you to get in the throwing position easier and quicker.

Moments before the ball goes into the glove, the other hand should be over it ready to be placed on top of the ball to prevent it from bouncing out, then to grab the ball and throw it. When the ball reaches the glove, create some give in the glove by bringing the glove up towards your stomach. This movement creates a soft landing area for the ball, or what I call "soft hands." You are trying to keep from creating any tension in your hands or body when fielding the ball. Tense hands with no give in the glove will usually result in the baseball bouncing out of the glove.

Once you've caught the ball, shift your legs so the front leg and shoulder are square to the target. Crow hop or step with your front toe pointed directly at your target and throw the ball with an overhand motion. If you fail to step towards your target, the possibility of throwing the ball off line increases. It is very difficult to step in one direction and throw accurately in another. Throw the ball with your fingers on top of the ball grasping four

◆

seams. Try not to throw the ball over the target's head. A ball thrown over the target's head obviously has no chance of getting caught. A low throw in the dirt has a possibility of being scooped up or at least gives the first baseman a chance to block the ball and keep the runner from advancing.

If a ground ball is hit to your right, pivot on your right foot and cross over with your left leg over the right leg. Keep your glove arm outstretched and as low to the ground as possible. Remember you can still bring your glove up on a bad hop more easily than you can lower it. Catch the ball with your glove thumb pointing down, plant your right leg and throw the ball overhand to first.

If the ball is hit to your left, pivot on your left foot and cross over with your right leg over your left leg. Keep your glove arm out reaching for the ball, even if you think you might not catch it. Always be prepared and in position to catch the ball in case you do have a play on the ball. Catch the ball with the glove thumb pointing up.

Get in the habit of diving for all balls you think you might have a chance of getting. If you happen to dive and knock the ball down, preventing it from going to the out-field, you are better off, because the outfielder will not have a chance to miss the ball.

Fielding a Slow-Hit Ball

Charge a slow-hit ball with your body under control and field the ball with the ball directly in front of you. Never attempt to catch a ground ball off to the side unless the ball is barely moving. If you attempt to catch the ball off to the side and miss it, it will roll into the outfield with all runners advancing. Keep the ball in front of you so that if you then miss it or it takes a bad hop, the runners will not be able to advance.

◆

Popups

If a ball pops up in the infield, catch the ball with the glove open over the shoulder of your throwing arm. This will allow you a clear path to see the ball all the way into your glove. Trying to catch the ball over the other shoulder prevents the glove from opening up properly and makes catching it with two hands more difficult. Always catch the ball with two hands.

Outfielder's Fly Ball

Catching a fly ball in the outfield is similar to catching a popup in the infield except that your shoulders should be lined up square to the target whenever possible. Catch the ball out in front of you with your weight going slightly forward so you can get your weight behind your throw more quickly to prevent a possible delay in throwing the ball to your target.

If a ball is hit over your right shoulder, step back with your right foot, then cross over with your left foot and run back for the ball, never taking your eyes off the ball. If it's hit over your left shoulder, cross over the other way. If you're a right-hander and the ball is hit to your left, catch the ball with your glove hand cupped and thumb up. If the ball is hit to your right, catch it with the thumb of your glove hand pointed down. If you are left-handed, do the reverse.

Outfielder's Ground Balls

Catch a ground ball in the outfield exactly as you would as an infielder. In Little League, do not try to catch the ball off to the side. If a ball takes a bad hop and gets by

◆

you because you were not in front of it, the results could be disastrous.

If you try to field the ball like an infielder and it takes a bad hop, you can simply knock the ball down and prevent the runners from advancing.

Catcher

The catcher on a Little League team is second in importance only to a pitcher. A catcher is in every play; the entire game revolves around him and the pitcher. Your catcher should be intelligent, a leader and not afraid to take command behind home plate. A catcher should let all of his infielders know how many outs there are after each out, let them know which bunt play they are using, let the shortstop know that he has the throw on a steal, and so on. He basically becomes a coach on the field.

A catcher should squat down with the weight on the balls of his feet. His right foot should be slightly behind his left foot if he is right-handed. The glove hand should be down outside and below the left knee to prevent the third base coach from seeing the signals to the pitcher. The throwing hand should remain behind the back so as to not get hit by a foul tip.

When the pitcher begins his windup, the catcher should shift his weight slightly forward to the balls of his feet and come out of his crouch ever so slightly to be in position to grab a slow-hit ball in front of him or to throw the ball to second in case of a steal.

Defensing the Bunt

If a hitter bunts the ball, the catcher should approach the ball with a small arc, so that he can scoop the ball up with two hands and position himself square to the target he is throwing to. Make sure to step toward the target, and be sure to have a clear path to first base before throwing the ball. Get in the habit of knowing where the runner is before throwing.

If the bunt is made with a runner on first base, scoop the ball up with two hands and throw the ball directly to the second base bag. It is the shortstop's job to be on second ready for the throw. Make sure you throw the ball in front of the shortstop, not behind him. Any ball that is thrown behind a fielder is unlikely to be caught.

Popups

When a popup is hit in the general vicinity of the batter's box, the catcher should immediately take off his mask and, while still holding onto it, locate the baseball. Once the baseball is located, throw the mask in the opposite direction than the one in which you are going to run to catch the ball. This will prevent you from drifting back and falling over your mask. When a ball is hit to the catcher, it will have a tendency to drift back towards the playing field because of the underspin. Turn your back to the playing field and proceed to the ball. The ball will automatically spin back towards you. Never attempt to catch the ball facing the playing field, especially if you are in fair territory. If a ball is hit so that you have to run out towards it in fair territory, it is best to let it be caught by another one of the fielders because it is easier for them to catch a ball drifting towards them than it is for the catcher to field a ball drifting away from him.

Blocking the ball

One of the main jobs of the catcher is to block all balls in the dirt. On low pitches in the dirt simply "drop and stop" the ball. Fall forward to your knees with the glove going to the space between your legs. Keep your head down, looking in front of you. Try to keep the ball in front of you. As soon as the runners on base see the ball in front of you, they will not attempt to advance.

If the ball is in the dirt to your right, stick your right leg out and slide your body until it is in front of the ball, then "drop and stop." If the ball is in the dirt, to your left, slide your left leg out and move your body until it is in the path of the ball. You are trying only to block the ball in this situation, not to catch it.

Pitcher Defense

After delivering the ball to home plate, the pitcher becomes an infielder. This is why it is so important for the pitcher to maintain good balance and be in the ready position after he has thrown the ball to home plate. The pitcher has to anticipate the ball coming right back at him.

If a ground ball has been hit to the pitcher with a runner on first base, he must make sure he leads the shortstop with the baseball right over the bag. Be careful not to throw the ball behind the shortstop; that makes it virtually impossible for him to stop his body's momentum, turn around and catch the ball. Always keep the ball in front of him so even if the throw goes wild, he can at least dive forward for the ball.

On any ball hit to the right side of the infield, toward the second or first baseman, the pitcher should automatically break towards first base to cover the base if the first baseman wanders too far off the bag.

Break towards a spot approximately 10 to 15 feet up the line from first base and then angle up parallel to the foul line to take the throw from either the first or second baseman. The ball should be fed underhand and aimed

◆

in front of the pitcher. This will make it easier on the in-fielders to make an accurate throw and give the pitcher enough time to catch the ball first and then touch the first base bag.

The pitcher should cover home plate any time a wild pitch or passed ball takes place with a runner on second or third. Never anticipate that the runner on second is going to stop at third base on a wild pitch. As pitcher, you should cover home plate facing the catcher awaiting the throw. Once the throw is made and caught, put your glove down on the ground and tag the runner in front of home plate. Make sure you do not catch the ball and at-tempt to tag the sliding runner after his foot has already passed over home plate.

First Baseman

The first baseman's main job is to catch the ball from the infielders to record an out. If the first baseman is left-handed, he should use his left foot to tag the base. If he is right-handed, his right foot would be easier to use to tag first base.

On ground balls wide of first base, the first baseman should attempt to get everything until called off by the second baseman. Knowing where the second baseman is, and which ground ball is whose, will take a lot of prac-tice. Once the first baseman catches the ball, if he is too far off of the bag to run over and tag the base before the batter gets there, he should lob the ball underhand to the pitcher, chest high. Be sure to get the ball to the pitcher before he reaches the bag if at all possible.

The first baseman should be alert on any passed balls or wild pitches to cover home plate if the pitcher forgets.

When a ground ball is hit with a runner on first base, throw the ball hard and accurately to the short-stop's chest.

Second Baseman

The second baseman has to cover first base on ground balls hit to the first baseman with runners on first for the double play. Anticipate a ground ball being hit to the first baseman with a runner on first. This will keep you alert so you won't be late in covering on that play.

The second baseman should catch any fly balls hit in foul or fair territory behind the first baseman that the first baseman has to struggle to catch. The angle on the ball off the bat is much easier for the second baseman to catch than for the first baseman.

The second baseman has to cover first base on bunt plays. Anticipate the other team bunting with a runner on first and get to the bag with enough time to set up normally and catch the ball. Make sure that your left foot is on the outside part of the bag. This gives the fielders a good target to throw at and also prevents the runner from stepping on your foot.

It's up to the second baseman to let the center and right fielders know how many outs there are after each out has been made.

Finally, the second baseman is the cut-off man on any balls hit past the outfielders on his half of the field.

Shortstop

The shortstop has to cover second base whenever a runner attempts a steal. Get to second base early and straddle the bag awaiting the throw from the catcher. Be ready for a bad throw.

Cover second base on a bunt with a runner on first. Time your move toward second so that the catcher will be throwing the ball over the bag at exactly the same moment you get there. This way your momentum will carry you toward first in case of a possible double play.

The shortstop should back up the catcher's throws back to the pitcher after every pitch, whether or not there is somebody on base. Backing up after every pitch will help the shortstop develop the habit, so he won't forget to back up when a runner is on base.

On fly balls, the shortstop takes priority when a ball is hit too far over the third baseman's head for him to handle easily. And of course, the shortstop is the cut-off man on any balls hit near the outfielders on the shortstop's half of the field.

The shortstop should let the outfielders know how many outs there are after each out is made.

Third Baseman

The third baseman should charge the bunts and field them with two hands, then make a strong, accurate chest-high throw to the intended base.

The third baseman should attempt to catch any ground ball hit to his left. It is much easier for the third baseman to field this ball than it is for the shortstop, since the shortstop will not have enough time to field it and still make a strong enough throw to put the runner out at first.

When there are runners on second or third, the third baseman should be alert for passed balls or wild pitches. He should also back up the pitcher in case the catcher makes a bad throw to the pitcher covering home.

Outfielders

The outfielders should always back each other up on all ground balls and fly balls that are hit to them.

◆

The right fielder should back up all balls thrown to first base.

The outfielders should always anticipate that the ball is going to be missed or go by an infielder so they will be in the correct position to catch the ball and get it back to the infield.

Throw the baseball chest high to the cut-off man on all cut-offs.

Back up all bases on any attempted steals or throws to the infielders from another infielder.

Keep your head in the game. Always anticipate what might happen before it does happen.

Basic Defense

Tagging a Runner

When you are chasing a runner, trying to tag him out, be sure to tag him with the ball in your glove. Having the ball in your glove gives you an extra two or three inches to reach for and tag him; it also prevents the ball from being knocked out of your hands.

When a runner is sliding into your base, make sure you are straddling the base awaiting the throw. Keep your knees bent and be alert for a possible bad throw. All too often when a bad throw is made, the fielder is not ready for it; if he were, he would be able to stop the ball from getting by him. Catch the ball out in front of you and immediately position the glove towards you on the ground directly in front of the bag. Do not try to actually tag the runner, but let the runner tag himself out by sliding into your glove. Once the runner is tagged, pull your glove up and out of the way to make sure the ball does not get knocked free. The fielder who tries to tag the runner often ends up tagging the runner too high up on his body after the runner is already safely back to the bag.

Defensing the Steal with Runners on First and Third

The runner on first base will attempt to steal second base in this situation for two reasons:

1. He believes he can steal the base easily because he thinks the catcher has been instructed not to throw the ball to second, but to hold onto it so the runner on third will not even attempt to come home on the throw.
2. He is trying to get the catcher to throw the ball to second so he can slow down before reaching the bag and get in a pickle. This will allow the runner on third a very good chance to score.

I personally use only two plays to defense this problem.

1. When the runner on first breaks to second, I will have my catcher throw the ball right to the bag, where the shortstop will catch the ball straddling the bag and tag the runner out.
2. If the runner on first breaks to second, have the catcher ignore him and throw the ball back to the pitcher.

A lot of teams have a myriad of plays they use trying to trap or fool the runner on third base into either breaking for home trying to score or wandering too far off of third base. They will try to trick the runner by having their catcher throw the ball to the shortstop or second baseman, who will immediately throw the ball home to get the unsuspecting runner.

I strongly advise against these plays because they will inevitably break down in one of several ways:

◆

1. The catcher may throw the ball wildly past the infielders, allowing all runners to score.
2. An infielder may drop the ball, allowing the runner on third to score and the runner on first to be safe at second.
3. An infielder may catch the ball and throw wildly to the catcher, allowing all runners to be safe.

Don't take any chances on a play that is very hard to execute. Either throw the runner out at second or throw the ball back to the pitcher and let the runner steal second. Remember, keep it simple and be sure you get one out. Make the other team earn their run by having to hit the ball.

The Rundown Play or "Pickle"

This is a play in youth baseball that usually ends with disastrous—and often hilarious—results. This play must be practiced until all the children understand the philosophy behind it.

In the rundown play, a runner is caught in no-man's-land, that is, off the bag between one bag and the other, with a fielder holding the ball and trying to tag him out. Let us use an example. Suppose you, the pitcher, are holding the ball and the runner is caught between third and home plate. The technique is always the same. Run directly at a spot in front of the runner, so he cannot advance to the base without being tagged out. Force him to retreat to the bag he was coming from. If you run him into the base he is trying to go to and you happen to make a bad throw or your teammate drops the ball trying to tag him out, he will be safe and one base closer to scoring. It is wise to run him back to the bag he just came from so that if he is safe at the base, no harm is done.

◆

Once you stop the runner's forward progress and are chasing him back to the original base, make sure the ball is out of the glove so your third baseman can see the ball and won't be surprised by a snap throw. It is also a lot simpler to throw the ball from this position than to reach into the glove to pull the ball out.

The general rule is: Keep the throws to a minimum. The more throws you do make, the greater the possibility of a mistake in which the runner ends up being safe. Have the third baseman straddle the bag awaiting the throw. Being on the bag instead of in front of it will prevent interference being called on the fielder. (Interference will be called if the runner makes contact with any fielder not holding the baseball.)

When the pitcher is chasing the runner towards third, be sure that the pitcher is outside the runner's lane so he does not throw the ball and hit the runner in the back. The throw should be made when the runner is in a position where he cannot reverse his direction once the third baseman has the ball. You should practice and strive for a one-throw tag on all rundown plays.

If the players cannot make the one-throw tag and the runner is able to change direction without being tagged, the pitcher should simply follow his throw to third base and take the third baseman's position as *he* chases the runner forward. The catcher should now come up the baseline, take the throw away from home plate and head the runner back to third. The third baseman should follow his throw and take the catcher's place in case the runner is able to escape again. If the catcher initiates the rundown play, make sure the pitcher or first baseman, whoever is closer, covers home plate. Be careful not to leave home plate unattended.

In other words, always follow your throw. What often happens is that a player does not follow his throw and the runner is able to run back to the unattended base. In Little League this usually means the entire team winds up in on the play and mass confusion ensues, with all members of the team yelling, "I got it!" Then the ball is thrown and all players simultaneously decide to let the other person have it. The ball then drops uncaught and all runners score.

This is just one example. The same choreography holds true no matter where the runner is picked off. Just remember to follow your throws and you will be all right. To work this play correctly, only three players are needed. Remember our motto: Keep It Simple, Stupid.

Relays and Cut-off

To Keep It Simple, we have changed the basic structure of relay throws for Little League and youth baseball because of the miniature size of the playing fields.

Instead of using a myriad of relay procedures, we use the pitcher exclusively as our cut-off man in the infield, no matter where the runners are. We are able to do this because of the size of the diamond and the almost nonexistence of any type of foul territory. On larger fields, where there is usually a large amount of foul territory, it is wise to use the first and third basemen as your infield cut-off players, with the pitcher backing up all throws.

On balls hit past the outfielders to the fence, split the field exactly in half. Most ballparks have a sign on the center field fence depicting how far is it from home plate to the fence. If you have one of those, use it as a guideline. If the ball is hit to the right of the center field sign, the cut-off man in the outfield is the second baseman. When the ball is hit to the left of the sign, the shortstop is the cut-off man.

The outfielders should try to hit the cut-off man on the glove side. Try not to throw the ball too hard to your cut-off man so you do not make it too difficult for him to run and catch it. If you miss the cut-off man, everybody will advance another base. If you hit the cut-off man correctly, the third base coach will notice this and stop his runners from advancing immediately.

◆

Each outfield cut-off player should get in position to catch the ball so he can turn his body in the direction of his glove hand. This will provide momentum to make a strong accurate throw and will also save valuable time getting rid of the ball.

The ball should be thrown low to home plate, ideally with one or two bounces. Never try to throw the ball all the way home on the fly: it is a lot easier to make a mistake trying to do that. If the throw is to second or third, the ball should be thrown directly chest high to the baseman.

Try not to throw the ball behind a runner on a cut-off play. This will make it easier for the runner to advance forward safely. Always throw the ball ahead of the runner to stop his forward progress.

The catcher or pitcher should call out to the outfield cut-off players where they want the ball thrown.

The infielders should make sure they are outside the baselines as they wait to see if they are going to be in the action or not. If they stand in the baseline watching what is transpiring in the outfield, they are liable to get run over by the runner. This will allow for interference to be called and possibly get the fielder injured.

The catcher should await the throw to home plate in front of the plate with his left leg blocking the baseline. If the throw is low, he must get down and block the ball so it will not get past him. If the throw is off line and is not picked off by the pitcher, the catcher should do whatever is necessary to stop the ball. If the ball gets by the catcher, the runners will advance at least one more base.

The pitcher as infield cut-off man should line himself up directly between the outfield cut-off player and the catcher. He must always let the ball go until the catcher shouts, "Cut" for no throw, "Cut 1" for a throw to first, "Cut 2" for a throw to second, "Cut 3" for a throw to third, or "Cut 4" for a throw to home. The infielders should all be ready straddling the bags awaiting a throw from the pitcher. If the pitcher does not hear anything from the catcher, that means the throw is on target and a play will be made at home plate.

Defending the Bunt Play

A great and often overlooked play on any level of baseball is the bunt. Defending the ball is equally important. No defensive play gets messed up as much as fielding a bunt in all of baseball, especially Little League. We start out All-Star practices with trying to defend the bunt with live bunting and fielding, and at least 70% of the time, the runner will be safe at first if the bunt is executed properly. You have to practice this play continually until everybody feels extremely comfortable and sure of what each player's role will be.

The Keep It Simple rule again comes into play. Do not try to make this any more complicated than it already is. Forget about having five or six bunt plays that are never executed correctly. Concentrate on two plays that all concerned will feel confident about.

With a runner on first base and less than two outs, always anticipate a bunt. Have your third baseman and first baseman cheat in toward the batter. Once the hitter squares to bunt the ball, the first and third baseman should charge the batter under control: After the ball is bunted, the catcher should call out who will take the ball. The person called should field the ball with two hands and throw the ball to the second baseman, who is covering first. The right fielder should be running to foul territory to back up any wild throws to first base.

I believe in using this alignment in all situations. You will find that if you keep this really simple for your kids, no mistakes will be made just because they don't know what to do.

The only other bunt defense play we work on is used when there are runners on first and second and there is a force play at third base—not a tag situation, a force play. Our pitcher and first baseman will then charge, trying to catch the ball and force the lead runner out at third. The shortstop and left fielder should back up the play at third in case there is an overthrow. The second baseman should cover first base in case the catcher realizes there is no chance of getting the runner out at third.

We will use this play only if the winning, not the tying, runner is on second in the last inning. I just do not believe it is worth the risk otherwise. Defensively, we are trying to eliminate, as much as possible, any chance of making a needless mistake. Having too many plays and making too many throws greatly increases the chance of something going wrong. Even if the tying or winning runner advances to third base on a successful bunt, there is still a chance of you getting two more outs before they do score. Keep it simple, and make the other team *earn* their runs.

The Double Play or Force-Out

The double play in youth baseball is a very difficult and very rare event. Our All-Star teams this year did make a number of very important double plays, but their skill level is probably a lot more advanced that that of most Little League teams. I do believe in practicing the play, however, because it teaches the importance of good footwork and hand dexterity.

When a double play situation develops, the second baseman has to be aware of his role. Once a ground ball is hit to the shortstop or third baseman, he proceeds to the base and puts his right foot on the bag with his left shoulder square to first base. He should make sure his knees are bent and stay alert for a good as well as a bad throw. So many times a second baseman is only ready for a perfect throw and if a throw is just a little off line, he is unable to catch it because he isn't in position for it. A second baseman should do everything possible to block an errant throw to keep it from going to the outfield. When the ball is on the way to him, the second baseman simply catches the ball with two hands, steps towards first base and throws the ball overhand. In Little League or youth baseball, this is the best and, again, the simplest way to make this play. Nobody is really trying to take out the second baseman or shortstop by sliding into him as players do in high school ball. Keep It Simple. Catch it and throw it. Do not make this game any more difficult than it is already. Everybody will be better off for it.

If the ball is hit to the pitcher, catcher, first or second baseman, the shortstop will cover second base. The shortstop should be alert and ready for a good or bad throw with his right foot behind the bag and his left foot alongside the bag. He catches the ball with two hands and drags his back foot across the bag with his momentum going toward first base, then throws the ball with an overhand motion.

The first baseman should field the ball if it's hit to him and attempt to hit the shortstop in the chest with his throw. The second baseman should rotate over in back of the first baseman and take the throw on the base. If the ball is hit at the first base bag, so that, after fielding the ball, the first baseman does not have to take more than two strides to tag the base, he should tag the bag and shout "Tag" to the shortstop. Once the first baseman tags the base, the force play is removed and the shortstop will have to tag the runner coming from first to put him out.

When a ball is hit to the second baseman or third baseman and it is within 10 feet of the bag, a shovel toss by the shortstop is called for. After fielding the ball within 10 feet of the bag, toss the ball underhand chest high with the weight traveling forward toward the front foot. The movement you want is akin to throwing a bowling ball in bowling. If you do not do this, it is a lot easier to make a mistake and throw the ball either straight up or too slow. You need to practice this play a lot to get your infielders used to each other's particular movements.

Ball in the Sun

When a ball is hit in the sun, place your closed glove directly in the sun so you have it completely blocked. Turn your body sideways to give the ball a smaller target to hit in case you never do see it. Look over the top of the glove and be ready to catch the ball when it comes out of the sun.

Regretfully, this is a tough one to practice. We really do not need any children going blind trying to learn the game of baseball. It is still useful to teach them what to do, though, in case they do get in that situation. If you use the correct method for blocking the ball from the sun and you still cannot see the ball, please remember to DUCK.

Popups in Foul Territory

When a ball is hit behind the first base bag in foul territory it's best to let the second baseman have it because he has a much better angle to catch the ball. In the same way, a ball hit over the third baseman's head in foul territory is the shortstop's ball.

Fly Balls Hit Between the Outfielders and Infielders

Practice hitting fly balls or even throwing them to a point between the infielders and the outfielders. Whenever possible, the outfielders should call off the infielders on plays like these. It is much easier for the outfielders to run in and catch these balls than it is for the infielders to make this play with their backs to the infield.

Team Positioning

In 1992 and 1993 in all-star play we made a lot of big plays that saved a number of games just by positioning our outfielders correctly. More than one great play took place when a ball was hit to one of our outfielders who just happened to be playing almost on the foul line.

We use one of three outfield alignments and a closed or open fist for shallow or deep. The first plan, the most common defense, involves playing all of your outfielders straight away—that is, with your center fielder directly in line with home plate and second base. Your left and right fielders should be equidistant from your center fielder, with the left fielder between second and third base and the right fielder between first and second.

In the number two defense, you are playing the outfield to swing over, or rotate, toward the left field line. The left fielder is now playing about 15 feet off of the line and the center fielder is rotated over so that he is in line with the second base bag and a point about halfway between home and first. The right fielder has moved over until he is in line with second and third base.

Number three has the right fielder rotated toward right field foul line and playing approximately 15 feet off of the foul line. The center fielder has rotated over to stand in a line with second base and a point about halfway between home and third. The left fielder has shifted over so that he is in line with first and second base.

Make sure the outfielders are all the same distance from each other. Do not put them too close or too far apart. You want them to be just far enough apart to be able to catch an average fly ball that is hit right between them.

The infielders should rotate also, but not quite to the same degree.

We use this alignment and strategy because we want to place our fielders where the ball is most apt to be hit. Makes sense. In youth baseball, I have found that if you have a pitcher who throws fairly hard, 90% of the time the hitter is going to be late swinging the bat. In other words, a right-hander will hit the majority of his pitches to the right side of second base. Conversely, a left-handed hitter will hit most balls to the left of second base.

Of course, you have to base your strategy on who is hitting, but generally our theory holds up. Play everyone to swing late.

We use a closed fist for playing at normal depth and an open hand for playing shallow. This decision depends on which hitters have power and which ones don't. If a hitter does not have the strength to hit the ball to the wall, don't play against the wall. If a hitter has home run power, play at normal depth. Never play *deeper* than normal on any hitter. You can always run back 30 feet to the wall to make the play. I see too many outfielders playing so deep that if they turn around to run after the ball they can take only about four steps before running into the wall. That is too deep. You will sacrifice too many balls that will fall in front of you for the rare ball that gets over your head.

Infield Depth

There are certain situations that require you to play your infield in to try to cut off a run at home plate. Play your third, second and first basemen and your shortstop in front of the baseline to stay out of any interference play. You'll be able to catch the ball and get it to home quicker than if you were playing normal infield depth. Never play at normal infield depth and attempt to throw the runner out at home. If you were going to make a play at the runner going home, you should have been playing in to begin with. If the ball is hit on the ground to an infielder with a runner on third and less than two outs, he should catch the ball and get the runner to stop advancing towards home, then throw the ball to first base. A word of caution: Never play in when there are two outs.

You might get to a point in a game where the winning run is on third base in the last inning with less than two outs. Play your infielders and outfielders in. If the hitter hits a normal fly ball, the baserunner is going to tag and score anyway. The outfielder will be able to catch the short fly balls that would otherwise drop in, and he can still throw the ball home to keep the runner from scoring.

Defense Philosophy

KEEP IT SIMPLE. This sums up my entire philosophy for playing defense. Keep it simple and you will be way ahead of the game. Play good, solid fundamental defense and make the other team earn their runs. Do not give them any cheap runs by trying the impossible or even the improbable while you are on defense.

Play for one out at a time. Avoid at all costs those situations where your kids think they MIGHT have a play to get an out. Be SURE that you are going to get an out before you throw the ball. If you do not think you will definitely get an out by your play, do not throw the ball.

Let's use an example of what can happen if you decide to try the iffy play: bases loaded, two outs and the runner on third leading off a little too far (according to the catcher). The catcher attempts to throw the runner out because he thinks he has a chance of getting him, but the ball on its way to the third baseman hits the runner in the back and caroms out into left field. The left fielder picks the ball up, thinks he can get the runner at second base out and proceeds to fire the ball to second. But the throw is too high, and the ball carries all the way over the second baseman's head to the first baseman. Now the first baseman thinks he can get out the runner who is trying to advance to third. He throws the ball low, in the dirt, the third baseman misses the ball, and all three runs score.

If these players had been taught to Keep It Simple, get one out at a time and take no chances unless they are SURE they can get an out, this disaster would have been averted.

One more time: Keep It Simple—and practice all of these situations as much as possible.

Practice

Let's face it. Nothing is more boring to kids than a conventional practice, no matter what the sport. A coach's job is to find a way to keep the kids interested and having fun while in the process teaching the kids how to play the game.

A normal practice usually consists of an infield practice followed by a lengthy batting practice. About halfway through the batting practice is when the kids start getting antsy and stop paying attention. You have to keep the kids busy. The attention span of young kids is not very long.

In order for these kids to participate in a learning atmosphere, the most important tool in learning is having fun. If we can provide a situation in which the kids are having fun playing baseball, they will learn at an incredibly faster rate than they would if they were trying to learn the old way. How do we make this happen? By playing games.

Our method of practice over the last few years has been the single most important reason for our success.

We provided the kids with the opportunity to play games in a competitive atmosphere and to learn baseball in a situation that is great fun for children. When you do that, you will find the kids looking forward to the next practice instead of figuring out an excuse not to go.

This is not to say that fundamentals are not important and can be overlooked. Quite the contrary, fundamentals should be stressed at every practice. Just make sure you leave yourself enough time to play your games.

Practice Schedule

I believe that you should practice at least three times a week for 1½ to 2½ hours. During our regular season with Long Beach Little League, our team, the Pirates, would play baseball four times a week. If we had one game, we would practice three times, and if we played three games, we would practice only one time. Everybody knew that we would be playing baseball four times a week, no matter what. It is also a good idea to give parents a schedule outlining the times of the games and practices.

Below is a sample practice schedule that I think would work out quite well.

Practice

4:00 P.M.—Stretch and run to get the muscles loose

4:15—Catch
When you have your kids play catch at every practice, be sure that they loosen up well and then start backing away from each other so they are constantly stretching their arms out. Start them out about 40 feet away from each other and then move back to 60 feet. After a couple minutes at 60, move farther back to 80 feet. This is a

good way for their arms to get stronger. Throwing the ball from 40 feet and never stretching it out is just going through the motions. Make every minute count while the kids are out there on the field.

4:25—*Fundamentals*

Fundamentals should be worked on at every practice. You have to teach the children the correct way of playing baseball from the ground up. Do not take it for granted that they know what to do. You have to remind them constantly of the right way to catch the ball, the right way to throw the ball, and the right way to hit the ball at every practice. This is how they are going to learn. If you don't correct the players the moment they make a fundamental mistake, they will think the way they are doing it is the right way. Don't let them practice with bad mechanics.

When you are practicing one of the fundamental drills, keep it short. The drill does not have to last a half hour. Go over it a few times with every player on the team and then move on to something else. Keep everything fresh.

The fly ball and ground ball drill should be used at every practice for just five minutes a day. This will reinforce the proper mechanics of catching and throwing the ball that the coach is trying so hard to teach. If you do these drills daily, after a short time you will begin to notice some marked improvement in the players.

4:45—*Defensive plays*

Form an infield with a child at every position except for pitcher. Hit three fly balls to each outfielder and have them throw one ball to second, third and home. Have each outfielder field three ground balls and throw one to second, third and home. Start off the infield portion of the practice by having the infielders simulate a bases-loaded force-out situation at home plate. Hit them three balls apiece and have them throw them to the catcher. Hit three balls to each infielder and have them throw

◆
89

them to first base. On the last ball hit to each infielder, have the catcher throw the ball back to first base after receiving it from the first baseman. Then have the players throw the ball around the infield with each infielder straddling the bag and tagging out an imaginary runner. Work on the double play twice with each infielder, emphasizing accurate throws to the second baseman and good footwork by the pivot man.

Finish the infield by hitting one slow ground ball to each infielder so that he has to charge under control to make the play.

Once you've finished this infield practice, move on to some game simulations, which you'll find in chapter 6. Be sure to include all your players in every infield practice, not just the starting lineup.

5:30—Intra-squad game

Every practice should always have at least 45 minutes set aside for your intra-squad games. These will be the heart and soul of your practices. If your team is made up of 12 ballplayers, split the teams into three groups of four. If you have more than 12 on a team, divide them up evenly.

During all-star play, we had 14 players on our team which made it real easy to split up the squad into two seven-man teams. Make sure all groups are as even as they can get in terms of ability. I say this because even if you tell them that you are not going to keep score, the kids will still keep score themselves. If one group is constantly beating the other group, the kids will start to complain about it, making your life miserable. So make them as even as possible. Be sure to have either the manager or coach pick the teams. Do not let two of your own kids pick the teams as so often happens. These two captains will probably pick their teams with regard to ability, best going first, second best second, etc. This will result in a negative experience for the kid that is picked last. It will reinforce the assumption that he is not very good or he would have been picked sooner. He probably already has doubts about his ability and they are now confirmed by this selection process. Your job as coach is to make sure each player is fed as much positive rein-forcement as possible, making sure that child feels great about himself. Getting picked last hardly boosts a child's self-esteem.

Now you have three groups of four children. The next step is to find two parents or coaches who will pitch and catch. Having parents pitching and catching during these daily games speeds up the practice because you do not have to wait for a kid to change in and out of the catcher's equipment. It also protects the catcher from possible injuries over the course of these intra-squad games. A parent needs to pitch because he or she usually has much better control than the children. Pitching prac-tice for the kids should only take place on the sidelines during practice and in the games.

Two years ago, my coaches talked me into having a regular intra-squad game with the kids pitching. I was against the idea at first, but after they explained to me how beneficial this would be to our pitchers and hitters, I grudgingly relented. We began the game and the first batter was my son. The first pitch our pitcher threw in the practice game hit him directly on the Achilles ten-don, and I thought he was seriously hurt. Luckily he wasn't, but that was the end of children pitching in our intra-squad games for good. It is so much safer if the parents pitch, and the kids will have more confidence in themselves knowing the adult has good control and will probably throw strikes.

Start with one group playing in the outfield. Having four players in the outfield is not going to hurt anything, especially when all groups have to play the outfield in their rotation. The second group will be playing the infield. Try to keep the kids at the same positions at the practice that they will be playing in the game. The more familiar and comfortable they get at one particular position, the better they will perform and the more fun they will have.

◆

Too many times, I see coaches changing the kids' positions every inning. The kids will never have any self-confidence if this is done. They will be presented with too many decisions to make and not enough experience in any one position to know what to do. It would be like going to school and trying to learn five or six different musical instruments at the same time. The child will learn more and have a lot more fun if he just learns one instrument. The same holds true in learning a position. Keep it as simple as you can.

The third group will be up to bat. The game will be played just as it would if it were a regular season game. Strikeouts, hits, errors, etc. Four kids on one team is a minimum because if you have the bases loaded, you will still have a child left at bat instead of having to wait for one of the runners to run in and hit. It saves a lot of time. When three outs are made, the group that was hitting moves to the outfield and the outfielders come in to take up positions in the infield. The infielders are now up to bat and the game continues. When the new group has three outs, rotate again.

Play it just like you would a regular season game, with the exception of walks. Sometimes it is difficult to throw as many strikes as you would like, but the players don't need to walk. Once your hitter has been thrown four balls, start the count over with the same hitter remaining at bat.

If you are able to, have another parent coach third base, or first if you prefer, and get the children in the habit of looking to the coach for signs and help while they are running the bases. Play it just like a regular game. During the course of the intra-squad game, if one of your players does something wrong on the field, blow your whistle and stop the game. Explain to everyone what the child did wrong and how to correct it. Be sure to phrase your explanation in positive, encouraging terms; remember, a child who feels angry or humiliated as a result of his mistake won't learn a thing from it. In the same way, if a player makes any fundamental mistakes, such as throwing, catching, hitting or baserunning, take the time to correct them right then and there. This is the easiest, quickest and most enjoyable way for kids to learn the game of baseball, by playing under realistic conditions.

I cannot emphasize enough how important it is to include these intra-squad games in every practice. During the last two years of all-stars, not one practice went by that we did not use this method. It worked so well that we either played or practiced almost every day for 2½ months, and the kids were still enjoying themselves at the end because they were having fun. Because we had played our games so frequently, the kids were presented with just about every situation you could possibly encounter in a baseball game and they were ready for it because they had done it so many times before. Our kids were just more experienced than a lot of the teams we played for this reason. The games make it enjoyable, not only for the children but the parents as well.

6:15—Pitching practice
You should work on pitching every day at practice. The only way your players are going to learn how to pitch is to do it. You can't work on your pitching when you are playing regular games. Time must be spent at practice on all the pitching fundamentals.

Have each catcher put his equipment on and catch for your pitchers for 10 or 15 minutes just to familiarize your catchers with your pitchers. Be sure to go over all the correct fundamentals with your pitchers to ensure that everybody is using the proper mechanics.

Alternate the kids at every pitching practice to make sure everyone gets a chance.

6:30—Practice ends
You have probably noticed that there is no time set aside for batting practice. Batting practice should be taken be-

◆

fore regular season games only. There simply is not enough time in the practice schedule to have batting practice. We want to practice as efficiently as we can. Using a lot of practice time for batting practice does not make much sense to me.

Batting practice is boring to everyone except the player who is hitting. Everyone else usually just stands around and shags balls. If a player needs extra batting practice, have his parents or a friend throw to him when he has time on his own, or suggest he spend some time in the local batting cages if he is fortunate enough to be close to one of them.

Game Day Preparation

Have your team report 1½ hours before the game to take some batting and fielding practice. Batting practice before games will get their bodies and minds ready to hit once the game begins.

Divide the kids into three groups and alternate.

1. Batting practice. Each hitter gets eight swings.
2. Shag the baseballs. The kids should collect the balls from batting practice and get them back in to the coach.
3. Catch fly balls and ground balls from a coach.

When one group is done, simply switch them with one of the other groups.

Let's say this procedure is adhered to over the course of an entire season that lasts 24 games. Figure that if you get eight swings per practice times 24 games, you will have taken 192 more swings than you would have if you had not had batting practice. If each kid fielded 20 balls during the fielding part of this schedule, in 24 games he would have caught 480 more baseballs than if he had not done this. WIth this kind of repetition, I guarantee you the players will improve over the course of a season.

Due to a lack of fields in most areas, there are not many places where you can safely take batting practice. We solved this problem by going out and making our own portable backstop. It consisted of PVC pipe and a screen made by a local fishing net company. When the practice was over, we simply took it apart, folded it up and carried it away.

We also made a protective pitching screen that we could hide behind when the kids were hitting. This saved a lot of sore spots on our bodies over the years by shielding us from some hard-hit line drives.

Game Strategies

During the course of a game many decisions must be made. Here are some practical hints that I think you will find quite useful.

1. Lead off your lineup with your best hitter and go down in descending order in terms of ability. This will provide your best hitter with as many chances to get up to home plate as possible. Try to arrange it so the last player in the lineup isn't made to feel worthless, though.

2. Coach third base. If their dugout is on the third base side, some teams like to put their one allowable grown-up coach on first base because they feel they will be able to communicate with the runner on third base from the dugout. I personally don't think it works very well. There are just so many

split-second decisions that have to be made
from the third base coaching box that you have
to put your adult coach there to keep the lines
of communication between the baserunner and
coach open as much as you can. You just cannot
coach your baserunners from the dugout.

3. Calling pitches. At the more advanced level,
I think it is a good idea for the coach to call
all pitches. For the most part, the coach just
has more experience in game situations
than the child has. By watching the hitters
you are able to tell whether or not to throw a
fast ball or an off-speed pitch by the way the
hitter stands or swings. A few tips would be:

a. Hitter is taking great swings at a fastball.
Throw a curve.

b. Hitter is late on a fastball. Throw a fastball
inside.

c. Hitter is pulling the ball foul. Throw an off-
speed pitch.

d. Hitter stands too close to home plate. Throw
fastballs inside corner.

e. Hitter stands far away from home plate.
Throw either fastballs or curveballs on the
outside of home plate.

f. Hitter holds hands low. Throw fastballs
above his hands.

g. Hitter holds hands high. Throw fastballs
down low in the strike zone.

h. Hitter has a 3-1, 3-2 or 2-0 count on him.
Always throw a fastball. You can control a
fastball a lot better than a curveball. You
are trying to stay away from walking anybody if at all possible. If the score is tied, a
strong hitter is up and first base is unoccupied, you might want to throw him a curveball here to possibly prevent him from
hitting the ball; a walk will not kill you in

this situation. Ninety percent of the time, however, throw a fastball and try to stay away from walking anybody.

5. With the count 0-2, try to hit the outside corner or waste a pitch to try to get the batter to go after a bad pitch.

6. If you have a pitcher who throws hard, shift your defense to play the hitter to hit the opposite way. Let's say a right-handed hitter is up. Shift your defense towards the right field foul line. If it's a left-hander, shift your defense towards the left field line. This will put your players in the right position to catch a ball hit late.

7. Do not scream at your players if they make a mistake. Just offer some constructive criticism. Be positive at all times. If the player makes a mistake on the ball field, wait until the inning is over and gently correct him. Explain what it is he did wrong and what he should do to correct it the next time. Yelling and screaming at him will only alienate the player and the player's parents. I have never met a child yet who intentionally tried to strike out or miss the ball. Everybody makes mistakes. Your job is to help them and be positive. Keep the children in a good frame of mind so when they have another chance they won't be scared to death to attempt the play.

Drills

Defensive Drills

Position five kids at second base and five kids at short-stop. One player should be on first base and another one should be on third base.

Have the coach line up on the third base side and hit a ground ball to the player on second. Have him throw the ball to third base using all the proper fundamentals.

Have the coach line up on the first base foul line and hit a ground ball to the shortstop. Have him throw the ball to first base utilizing all the proper fundamentals.

Make sure that the players are using the correct fundamentals every time a ball is hit to them.

Ground Ball Drill

The kids should pair off and get approximately 40 feet from each other. One player should throw the ball on the ground with the other player concentrating on all the fundamentals. Stay in front of the ball, get low, hands out front, catch the ball, bring it into your chest, square, step toward the target and throw it overhead. After about a dozen grounders, the kids switch and the one that was catching the ball starts throwing balls to the other player.

This method of pairing up will dramatically increase the chances a kid will have of fielding a ground ball compared to the regular way of just hitting the ball to each individual and then having each go wait in line until the rest of the team has gotten a chance to field.

Make sure you constantly remind the kids of the correct fundamentals every time they field the ball. This is what this drill is for: to hammer into the kids the proper mechanics of fielding the ball.

Toss Drill

This is just like the above drill except the players are closer together. Have the children pair up and get about fifteen feet away from each other. They should practice both the underhand soft toss and the overhand toss to simulate the double play or force-out.

Throw the underhand soft toss as you would a bowling ball. If you are right-handed you should toss the ball with your left foot leading your body. Be sure to transfer your weight forward to prevent you from throwing the ball straight up in the air.

Throw about a dozen grounders to each other and then switch.

This will teach them exactly how hard they are able to throw the ball and still be able to control it.

Double Play Drill

Have two or three kids play short and second base. Have them alternate every grounder. Hit a ground ball to the second baseman and have him catch the ball correctly.

He should pivot and throw the ball either underhand or overhand, depending on how far away he is from the bag. The shortstop should practice dragging his right foot over the bag and throwing the ball to first base. Work on hitting the ball to the second baseman and shortstop at all different angles and depths to get them comfortable with all the different plays needed.

After a dozen or so, shift over and hit the shortstop some grounders, and have him practice his feeding to the second baseman. The second baseman should work on his footwork around the bag and throw the ball to first base.

These drills will provide the players with an opportunity to work on their footwork and to familiarize themselves with how hard they should throw the ball to each other.

Pitchers' Drill
(Covering First Base and Forcing the Runner at Second Drill)

Position your pitcher, shortstop and second and first basemen in their normal spots. Either hit a ball right back to the pitcher and have him complete the force-out at second base or hit the ball wide of the first baseman and have the pitcher cover first base.

If the ball is hit back to the pitcher, make sure the pitcher turns toward his glove hand and leads the shortstop with his throw. Time the throw so that the ball is going over the base in front of, not in back of, the shortstop. The shortstop should work at pacing himself so he can catch the ball the moment before he touches the bag.

If the ball is hit to the right side of the infield, the pitcher should automatically break as soon as the ball is hit so he will be covering first in time. You have to do

◆

this drill frequently until the pitcher understands that the moment the ball is hit to the right side, he must break towards first immediately. A two-second delay in breaking to the bag will result in the baserunner beating the pitcher to the bag. The pitcher should run to a spot approximately 10 feet in front of the bag and arc his path to create a better angle to catch the ball. The first baseman should use either the soft toss or overhand toss, depending on how far he is from the bag, and throw it in front of the pitcher before he gets to the base. This will enable him to concentrate on catching the ball before he has to figure out where the bag is.

This drill also enables the first and second basemen to work on communicating to each other who will field the ground ball. If the second baseman feels that he can handle it, he should call the first baseman off of the ball and let him remain on the base. The pitcher should still automatically break toward the bag even if the ball is hit to the second baseman.

Bunt Drill

Line the players up in front of the third base line and roll a slow bunt toward them. Have the players charge the ball with an arc so they can position themselves at a better angle to pick the ball up with both hands and throw the ball to first.

Outfielders' Overhand Drill

Position the outfielders in center field and place the infielders over by third base. Make sure their arms are loosened up. Hit either a ground ball or fly ball to each outfielder and have him catch it using all the proper fundamentals. Then he should take two to three steps, or crow-hop directly at his target, and throw the ball overhand with two fingers on top of the ball. Try to hit one or two balls that bounce in front of the fielder. Make sure the ball bounces out far enough in front of the infielder so it is easy to catch. Avoid short-hopping the infielder by bouncing the ball in the dirt too close to him, thus making it very difficult to catch. I would much rather have the ball bounce three times before it gets to the infielder rather than short hop to him. Most short hop throws are so hard to handle that the ball will inevitably get by the infielder and will let the runners advance.

If it's thrown overhand the ball will go farther and straighter than it would if you were to throw it sidearm or even three-quarters. The ball will also skip straight towards the target, and not bounce to the left or right, if it is thrown in this manner.

Outfielders' Fly Ball Drill

Have a coach stand approximately 60 feet away from the outfielders. Alternate throwing the ball over the right and left shoulders and directly over their heads. Throwing the baseball is easier than trying to hit it because you can place the ball pretty close to where you want it to go. If the ball is over the outfielder's right shoulder, the first step he makes should be a drop step with his right foot and then crossover with the other leg. If the ball is over his left shoulder, he should drop step with the left foot and then crossover with the right leg.

On normal fly balls, catch the ball in front of you in the space between the head and throwing shoulder whenever possible. Position your body so that your feet are spread shoulder width apart and your weight or momentum is going slightly forward. Getting your momentum moving slightly forward will help power your throws back in toward the infield, or in this case, to the coach.

At all costs, avoid trying to catch the ball while backpedalling. Try to catch everything in front of you.

When they are running after the ball, make sure the kids are running on the balls of their feet. Running on the balls of their feet should steady their running movement to prevent the fly ball from seeming to bounce up and down while they are running, making it easier for them to catch the ball.

Catch the ball with two hands, if possible. No basket catches unless there is no other way. After catching the ball, square your body and step towards your target. Throw the ball overhand with your fingers on top of the ball.

Outfielders' and Infielders' Communication Drill

Position one infielder in the shortstop position. He will form an imaginary triangle with the two outfielders on the left side of the diamond.

Have the second baseman play his normal position with two more outfielders behind to form a triangle. Make sure the spacing between all three of them is a little closer together than normal playing distance.

Throw or hit a baseball toward the fielders, alternating between the outfielders and the infielders. Have the outfielder or infielder who is about to catch the ball shout "mine" before he catches it to let the other fielders know when to clear out of his way. The other fielders should shout "yours" when they realize that he is in a better position to catch the ball than they are. The outfielder, after acknowledging his teammate by shouting "yours," should run behind him to back him up in case he misses the ball.

◆

To speed up the drill, as soon as you are done throwing or hitting one ball to the left side, turn and proceed to do the exact same drill to the right side of the infield.

After you have each group field a dozen or so balls, alternate the other kids in so that everyone has a chance.

This drill will teach all the kids the need to communicate properly. There is not a play in baseball that gets messed up as much as this one does. Work on this play at least once a week to keep the lines of communication open between the kids. The more you practice this drill, the better the kids will understand what it is that they are supposed to do and will make this play in a regular game.

Outfielders' Charge Drill

Line up the kids approximately 90 feet from the coach. Hit a ground ball to them so that they have to charge the ball and scoop it up outside their glove hand's foot. If you throw right-handed, you will be catching the ball outside and slightly in front of your left foot. If you are left-handed, the reverse is true.

After catching the ball, square your body, step towards your target and throw the ball to the coach.

Catchers' Drills

Catchers' Drop and Stop Drill

Position the catcher 40 feet or so from the coach and practice blocking balls in the dirt and off to each side. On balls directly in front of the catcher, have him drop immediately to his knees and place his glove and free hand in the slot between his legs to prevent the baseball from going through them. The catcher should keep his hand down and should not try to catch the ball, just block it and keep the ball in front of him.

The catcher must try to keep his body square to the pitcher to provide a bigger backstop for the ball to hit.

The catcher must get used to his equipment and realize that the ball is *not* going to hurt him.

Throw balls to the catcher's left or right and have him practice shifting his right leg out for balls to his right and his left leg for balls to his left. After shifting, he should drop and block the ball just like the drill above.

Catchers' Stance, Footwork and Throw Drill

The purpose of this drill is to work with the catcher on his stance, footwork, and throw on an attempted steal.

The catcher should get in this stance any time a runner is on base.

Instead of squatting and resting on your haunches, you have to come out of that a little and crouch a little more with your weight on the balls of your feet. Your right foot should be a little behind the left.

Throw the ball to the catcher in a full crouch and have him catch the ball while shifting his right foot behind him. This will square up his shoulder, hip and knee so he is in a perfect position to throw the ball to second base.

Grip the ball with four seams just like a pitcher, take one step and throw the ball overhand with your fingers on top of the ball and your weight shifting toward the target.

You must throw the ball overhand to second base to prevent the ball drifting to the right. If the throw happens to take one bounce (that's okay), it will skip straight because you have thrown the ball overhand.

◆

108

Catchers' Foul Ball Drill

Have the catcher in full gear facing the pitcher. Stand behind him and throw the ball as high as possible in foul territory.

Once the ball is thrown, holler "go!" and have the catcher immediately take off his mask and find where the baseball is. Once the baseball is located, have him throw the mask in the opposite direction, and catch the ball directly overhead with the palm up and fingers pointing towards him. He should not try to catch these balls in the basket style.

Pitching Drills

There are not many drills you can go through with the pitchers other than just practice throwing with their catchers. Pitching practice is still essential, though.

At every practice, two or three players should practice their pitching. You must practice to improve. A lot of youth baseball teams never practice their pitching and are disappointed if their pitchers do not do well in the games. Be sure to spend just as much time practicing your pitching as you would the other aspects of the game.

When practicing, stress the proper fundamentals and mechanics listed in the pitching section.

Hitting Drills

These drills are for one reason only: to teach the proper fundamentals and mechanics of the baseball swing. You must constantly keep reminding the players of the importance of learning and adhering to a good swing. Emphasize the correct way to hit and make sure you do not practice the wrong way. The more correct repetitions a young player performs, the quicker the body will understand exactly what it is that you are trying to teach it and the sooner he will start swinging properly in a game.

Soft Toss Drill

Have the hitter take his normal stance with a catch off to his side and slightly in front of him. Toss a ball softly in front of the hitter and have him proceed to swing at the ball driving it into a screen.

Be sure to concentrate on the mechanics of the baseball swing. We do not care how hard he hits the ball in this drill, we only care about his fundamentals.

Take your correct stance, set, attack stride, swing and follow through just like this book says to. Concentrate on pulling down your lead arm.

Lead Arm Soft Toss Drill

Perform this drill the same as above except use a small enough bat that kids can handle easily.

Take your normal batting stance and then drop your subordinate arm off of the bat, leaving just your lead arm gripping the bat. Toss the ball out front of the hitter and have him drive down and through the baseball. Stride and transfer your weight and follow through just like you would in a normal swing.

This drill will get your kids to understand the importance of your lead arm in the swing.

Flip Drill

Get a chair and a screen to protect you from any live balls that are hit back at you.

◆

Sit in the chair 30 or so feet in front of the hitter. Have the hitter take his normal stance and then get into the attack position ready to swing at the ball.

Flip him the ball over the plate and have him hit the ball with the correct fundamentals.

By being so close to the hitter, this drill will enable you to throw the ball to different spots: inside, outside, high and low. This will help the hitter learn the strike zone. You can also throw the ball to the hitter's weak spots to help him improve on those. You can also spin the ball to simulate a curveball and teach him the correct way to keep his weight and hands back.

By throwing the ball a little harder, you can show the young hitter why it is so important to be in the attack position before the pitch is thrown and not after. If he is not in the attack position, you will be able to throw the ball very easily right by him. Once he gets in the attack position, he should be able to hit the ball, thus reinforcing the importance of the attack position.

Hitting off of the Tee

Everybody knows what a tee is, but not everybody knows how important and beneficial a tee is to use. There is no greater teaching aid than a tee. Just make sure that you concentrate on all the fundamentals on every swing.

Pepper

Have one player with the bat and three fielders approximately 10 feet from him. Throw the ball to the hitter, who should hit it gently back to the fielders. The hitter should concentrate on keeping his hands above the ball when he begins his swing and swinging down or level to the baseball. He should try to hit a one-hop ground ball back to the fielders.

◆

After about a dozen or so hits, change positions with one of the outfielders.

Ground Ball Drill

Have a player take a bat and throw the ball up and hit it on the ground to an infielder about 50 feet away.

This is a simple drill, but it does teach the hitter that if he wants to actually hit the ball on the ground, he must keep his hands above the ball before hitting it, thus creating a proper swing through the strike zone. You cannot uppercut the baseball and hit a ground ball.

It also will create some good hand-eye coordination for the batter. It may sound simple, but throwing the ball up in the air and hitting it properly takes practice.

Sliding Drill

This drill should take place on some nice grass, not dirt, to protect the children from getting abrasions on their backsides and legs. Have the kids take their shoes off and line up in a line. When the coach says go, run toward the coach who is standing over the bag. Begin your slide in front of the bag and try to hook the bag with your lead foot. Have the kids really concentrate on hitting the ground with their hands in the air. Hold a batting glove in each hand to prevent you from jamming your hand or wrist into the ground.

◆

Game
Simulations

These defensive plays should be practiced at least twice a week up to 45 minutes per session. Use these diagrams to teach your kids what to do when the ball is hit to them. Each player should move to their spot every time a ball is hit. The more they practice these situations for every possible play, the more knowledgeable they will become and then they will understand what is expected of them. When one of these situations develops in a regular game, your kids will know exactly what to do because they have practiced it so many times.

Place your kids in the nine defensive positions. Have the rest of the kids put on helmets and be ready to run as soon as the ball is hit. The runners should run the bases just as they would in a regular game. Ask your defensive players "how many outs are there, where are the runners and what is the score?" before every new play. Hit the ball in a different spot each time with the baserunners running as soon as the ball is hit. After everyone has had a chance to participate in this drill, switch the runners with the fielders and continue.

1. These defensive plays are used for Little League or any other type of youth baseball where you are playing on small fields with little foul territo-

◆

115

ry. Because of the restricted foul territory, we use our pitcher for all cut-off plays at home plate. It is easier for kids this age to understand this method because there is somewhat less movement than in the normal way of executing cut-off plays at home. Since there is less foul territory in most Little League parks, if a person lets the ball get by him, it will not be able to go far since it usually bounces off the surrounding fence.

2. On all relays, balls should be thrown at the cut-off player's chest. The cut-off man should always turn his body to throw in the direction of his glove hand in order to gain momentum on his throws. All throws to a base should be kept low (one or two bounces), so the infielders or catcher can handle them easily; a throw over the infielder's head cannot be caught, thereby guaranteeing the runner's safety.

3. All infielders and catchers should always get down low in the dirt to block any ball thrown to them as soon as they realize that no play can be made at a base. Keep the ball in front at all times so the baserunners cannot advance.

4. Have your kids acquire the basic understanding of what is expected of them at just two positions, excluding pitcher. Keep it simple, do not confuse them with the task of learning a number of different positions. You might think you are helping them by exposing them to so many different spots, but you are actually hurting them by asking them to remember too much.

5. Utilize these drills to work on the kids' baserunning. If they happen to make a baserunning mistake, stop and show them what they should have done in that situation.

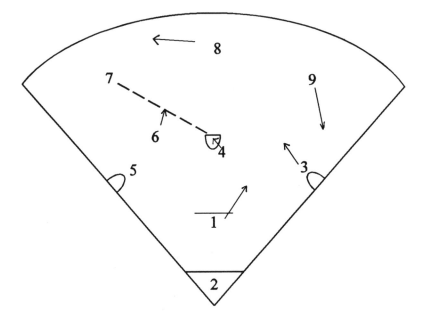

Nobody on base. Single to left field.

Throw the ball to the shortstop or second baseman, making sure the ball does not go over the second baseman's head. The right fielder and first baseman should back up the throw to the infield. You do not have to throw the ball as hard as you can, just get it in to the infield.

◆

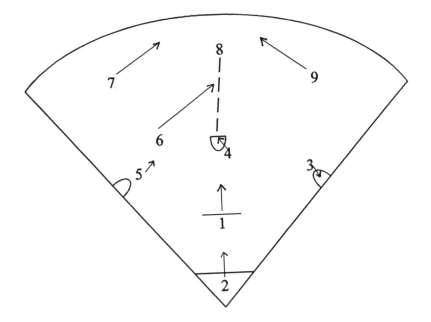

Nobody on base. Single to center field.

The ball is fielded and thrown gently back to either the shortstop or the second baseman.

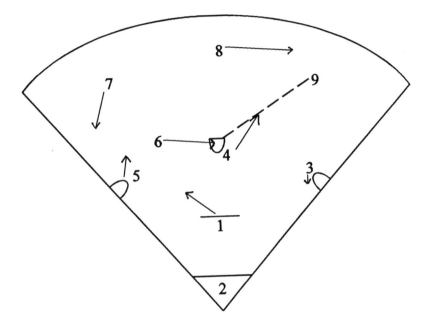

Nobody on base. Single to right field.

The left fielder and third baseman should back up the right fielder's throw.

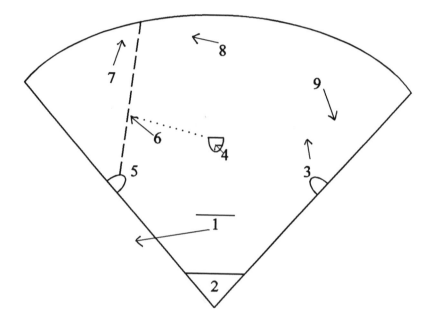

Nobody on base. Double to left field.

The ball should be thrown either on one bounce to the third base bag or to the cut-off man. The cut-off man should then look to second base for a possible pick-off play. The outfielders should back up all throws.

◆

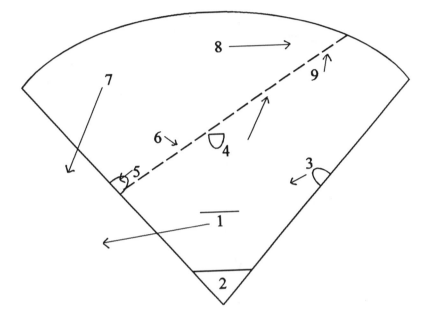

Nobody on base. Double to right field.

Ball should go to the cut-off man (second baseman) and be thrown low to third base. If the runner rounds the bag too far the shortstop will be ready for the pick-off play. If there is no play at third base the shortstop will cut off the ball.

◆

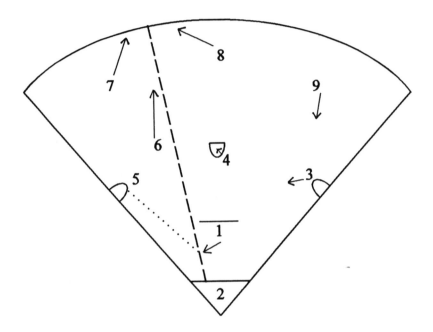

Nobody on base. Triple to left field.

Ball is fielded and thrown to the cut-off man, who throws the ball on one hop to the catcher. The pitcher, who is the second cut-off man, will cut off the ball if there is no play at home plate and run the baserunner back to third.

The third baseman stays alert and awaits a possible pickup throw from the pitcher. The left fielder hurries back and backs up the third baseman.

◆

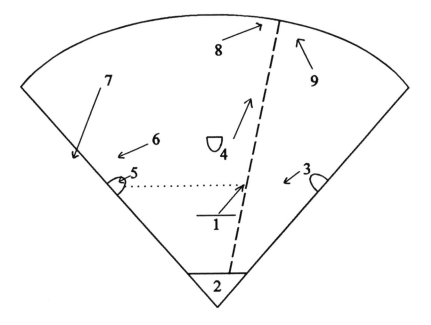

Nobody on base. Triple to right field.

Outfielder will pick up the ball and throw the ball to the cut-off man, the second baseman, who will then proceed to throw the ball on one hop to the catcher.

The pitcher will cut off the throw from the second baseman if there is no play at home plate, taking away the possibility of the throw getting by the catcher and allowing the runners to advance.

The left fielder will back up the third baseman in case of a throw to third by the pitcher trying to pick the runner off.

◆

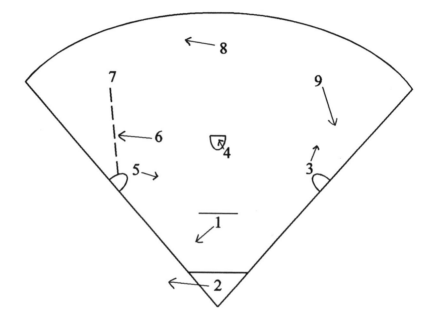

Runner on first base. Single to left field.

The left fielder should throw the ball on one bounce to the third base bag. The shortstop should go toward left field in case the ball gets by the left fielder.

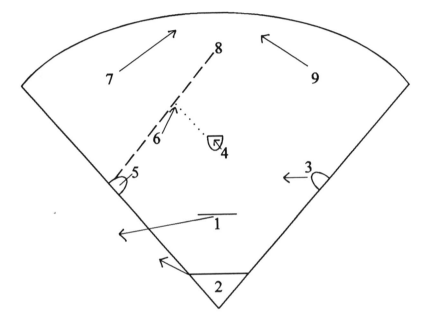

Runner on first base. Single to center field.

Shortstop should cut the ball off if there is a possible play at second. The right fielder and first baseman should be alert and ready to back up the play.

The center fielder should throw the ball on one bounce to the third baseman. The pitcher should back up the play behind third.

The center fielder should not throw the ball to third if he realizes that the runner will be safe at the base. The center fielder should then throw the ball to second, preventing the runner on first from advancing and keeping the double play or force-out in order.

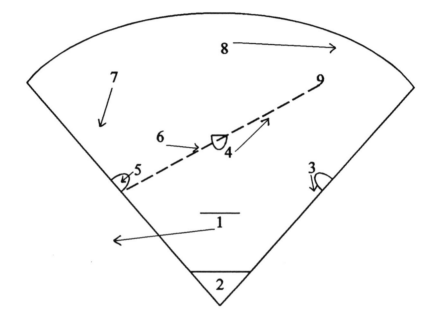

Runner on first base. Single to right field.

The right fielder should throw the ball on one or more bounces to third base. The second baseman should be out towards right field in case the ball gets by the outfielder.

The shortstop should cut the ball off if the runner stops at second. The pitcher and left fielder should back up third base. The shortstop should cut off the ball if there is no play at third base, preventing the runner from going to second.

◆

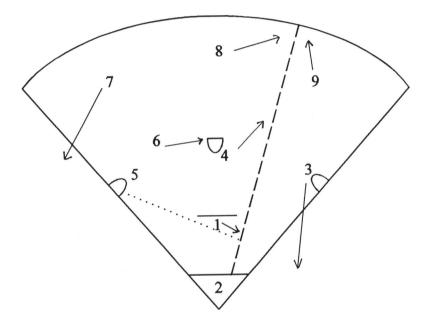

Runner on first base. Double to right field.

The outfielder will hit the cut-off man. The cut-off man will throw the ball with one bounce to the catcher. The pitcher will elect to cut the ball off if there is no play at home. The pitcher will then look at third and second for possible pick-offs.

The shortstop will cover second base and the left fielder will back up third base.

◆

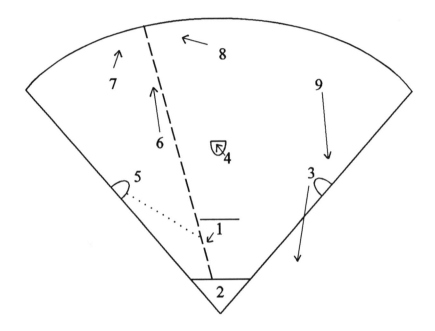

Runner on first base. Double to left field.

Outfielder will throw the ball to the cut-off man, who will throw the ball on one bounce to the catcher. The pitcher will cut off the ball if there is no play at home plate. The pitcher will look to see if there is a play at third base. The second and third basemen will be alive for a possible throw from the pitcher.

◆

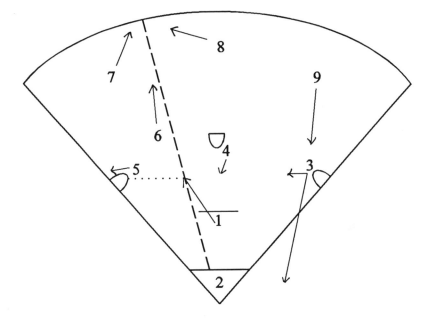

Runner on first. Triple to left center.

The left fielder or center fielder will field the ball and throw it to the cut-off man. The cut-off man will throw the ball on one bounce to the catcher. The pitcher will cut the ball if there is no play at home plate. The pitcher will throw the ball to third base if he believes he has a good chance to get the runner out.

◆

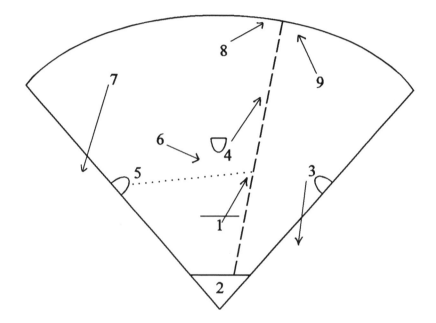

Runner on first. Triple to right center.

The outfielder will throw the ball to the cut-off man. The cut-off man will throw the ball on one bounce to the catcher. The pitcher will cut the ball off if there is no play at home plate. The pitcher will look to third for a possible pick-off play. The left fielder will back up the possible play at third.

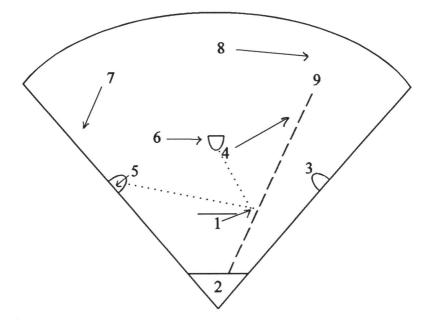

Runners on first and second. Single to right field.

The right fielder should throw the ball on one bounce to the catcher. The pitcher should cut off the ball if there is no play at home and look to third, second and first for a possible pickoff play. The outfielders should back up all bases in case of a pick-off throw.

◆

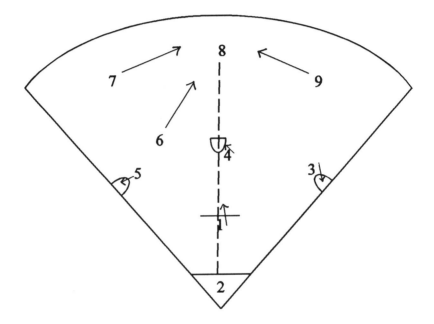

Runners on first and second. Single to center field.

The center fielder will throw the ball on one bounce to the catcher. The pitcher will cut off the ball if there is no play at home and look to third, second or first for a possible pick-off play.

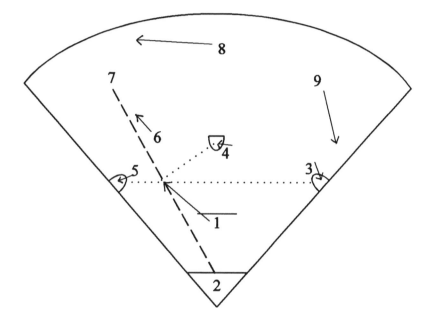

Runners on first and second. Single to left field.

The left fielder will throw the ball on one bounce to the catcher. The pitcher will cut off the ball and look to third, second and first for a possible pick-off play. The outfielders will be in position to back up all pick-off throws.

◆

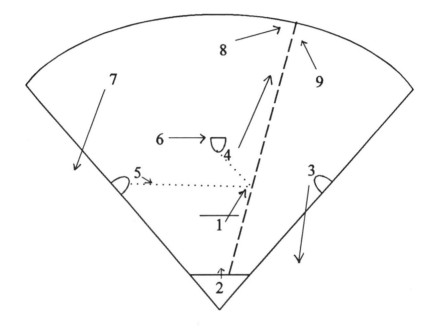

Runners on first and second. Double to right field.

The outfielder should throw the ball to the cut-off man who will then throw the ball on one bounce to the catcher. The pitcher will cut the ball off if there is no play at home plate and look at third or second for a possible pick-off play.

◆

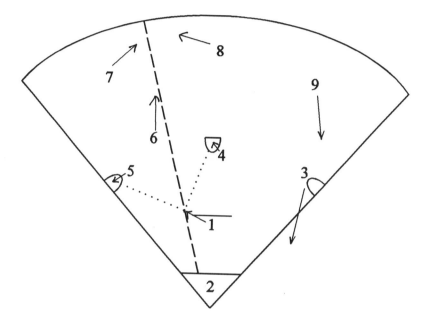

Runners on first and second. Double to left field.

The outfielder will throw the ball to the cut-off man who will then throw the ball on one bounce to the catcher. The pitcher will cut the ball off if there is no play at home plate and look to third or second for a possible pick-off play. Be careful on the pick-off at third because there is no backup.

◆

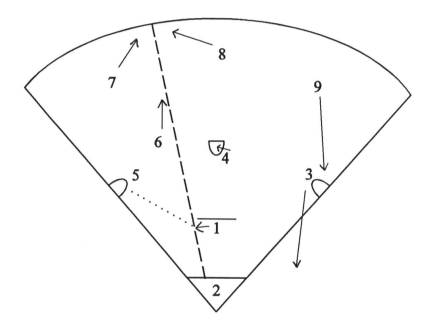

Runners on first and second. Triple to left center.

The outfielder will throw the ball to the cut-off man, who will throw the ball on one bounce to the catcher. The pitcher will cut off the ball if there is no play at home plate and look at third for a possible pick-off play.

◆

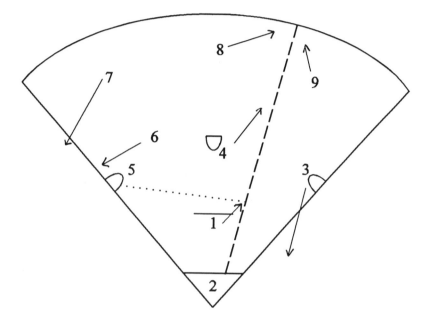

Runners on first and second. Triple to right field.

Outfielder will field the ball and throw to the second baseman. The second baseman will throw the ball on one hop to the catcher with the pitcher becoming the cut-off man.

The pitcher will cut off the ball if there is no play at home plate and look to third for a possible pick-off play.

The left fielder will back up the third baseman in case the pick-off throw gets by him.

◆

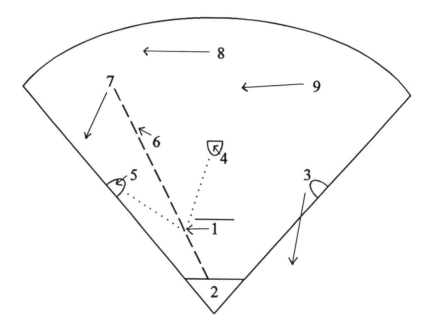

Runner on first, second and third. Single to left field.

Left fielder should throw the ball on one bounce to
the catcher. The pitcher should cut off the ball if there is
no play at home plate and look to third, second or first
for a possible pick-off play.

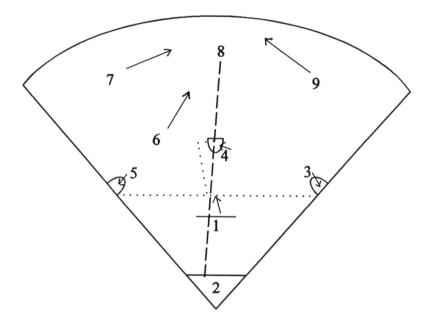

Runner on first, second and third. Single to center field.

The center fielder should throw the ball on one bounce to the catcher. The pitcher should cut off the ball if there is not a play at home plate and then look to third, second or first for a possible pick-off play. The outfielders should be in position to back up in case of a bad throw from the pitcher.

◆

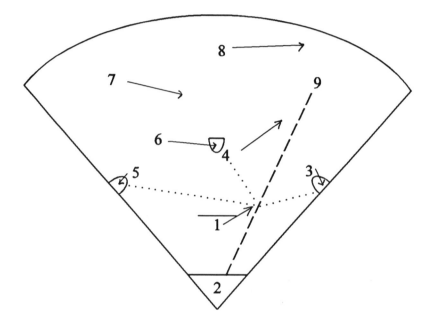

Runner on first, second and third. Single to right field.

The right fielder should throw the ball on one bounce to the catcher. The pitcher should cut off the ball if there is no play at home plate and then look to third, second, or first for a possible pick-off attempt.

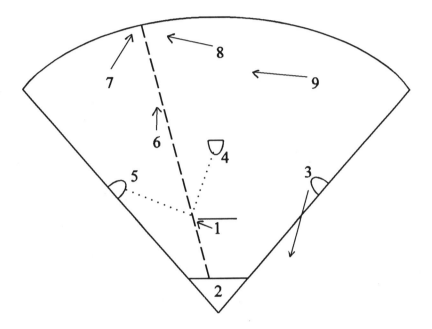

Runners on first, second and third. Double to left field.

The outfielder throws the ball to the cut-off man. The cut-off man will throw the ball on one bounce to the catcher. The pitcher will cut the ball off if there is no play at home plate and look at third and second for a possible pick-off play. The outfielders will back up the pick-off play.

◆

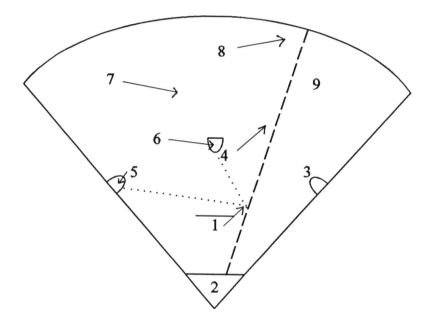

Runners on first, second and third. Double to right field.

The outfielder will throw the ball to the cut-off man. The cut-off man will throw the ball on one bounce to the catcher. The pitcher will cut the ball off if there is no play at home plate and look to third or second for a pick-off attempt. The outfielders will back up all throws.

◆

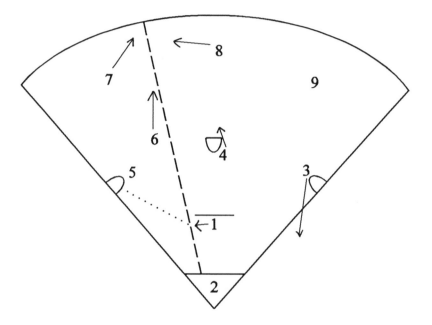

Runners on first, second and third. Triple to left field.

The outfielder will throw the ball to the cut-off man. The cut-off man will throw the ball on one bounce to the catcher. The pitcher will cut off the ball if there is no play at home plate and then look to third base for a possible pick-off attempt. The outfielders will back up all pick-off plays.

◆

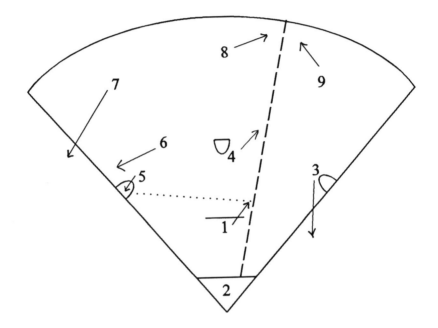

Runners on first, second and third. Triple to right field.

The outfielders will throw the ball to the cut-off man. The cut-off man will throw the ball on one bounce to the catcher. The pitcher will cut the ball off if there is no play at home plate and look to third for a possible pick-off attempt. The outfielders will back up all pick-off plays.

◆

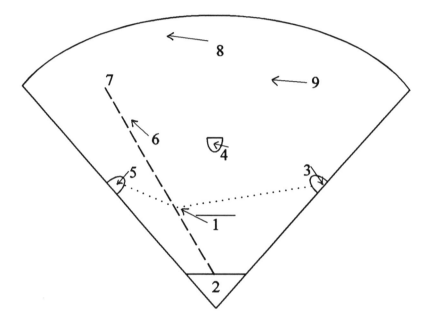

Runner on second base. Single to left field.

The left fielder will throw the ball on one bounce to the catcher. The pitcher will cut the ball off if there is no play at home plate and prevent the runner at first from advancing to second. The pitcher will look to first and third for a possible pick-off attempt. The outfielders will back up all pick-off throws.

◆

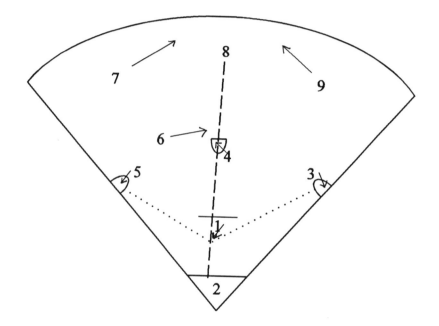

Runner on second base. Single to center field.

Same as single to left, except the center fielder makes the play.

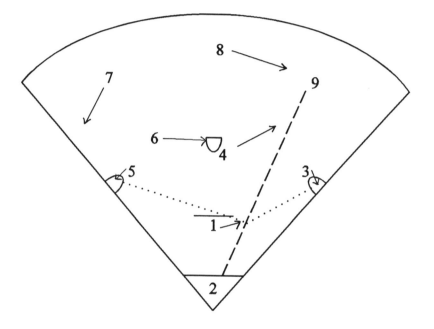

Runner on second base. Single to right field.

Same as single to left, except the right fielder makes the play.

◆

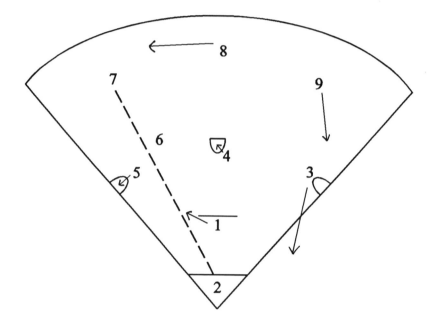

Runner on third base. Fly ball to left field with less than two outs.

The left fielder will throw the ball on one bounce to the catcher. The catcher will catch the ball in front of home plate to avoid a collision with the runner. He will catch the ball out front and tag the runner out.

◆

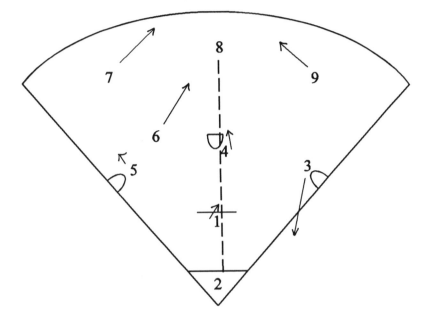

Runner on third base with less than two outs. Fly ball to center field.

Same as fly ball to left, except the center fielder makes the play.

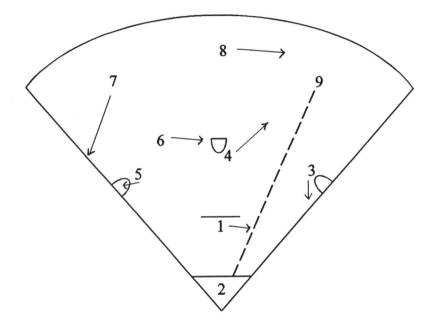

Runner on third base with less than two outs. Fly ball to right field.

Same as fly ball to left, except the right fielder makes the play.

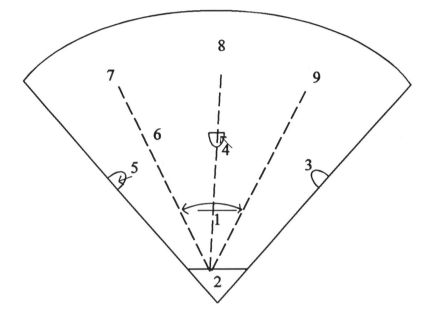

Runners on first and third, on first, second and third, or on second and third, and a fly ball is hit to any outfielder with less than two outs.

The outfielder will throw the ball on one bounce to the catcher. The pitcher will cut off the ball if there is no play at home plate. This will prevent the runners from advancing.

If the outfielders realize that there is no chance for a play at home plate, throw the ball to the base ahead of the most advanced baserunner to keep him from advancing further.

◆

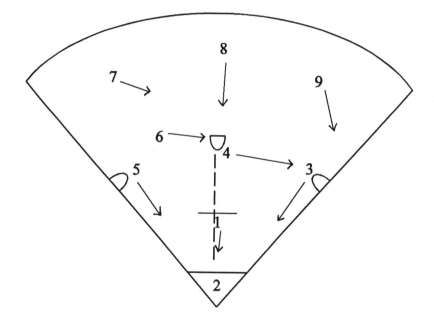

Runner on first base. Ball is bunted hard.

The catcher will yell two and the infielder will throw the ball to the shortstop covering the bag for a force-out. Be sure that this play can be made easily; if not, go for the easy out at first.

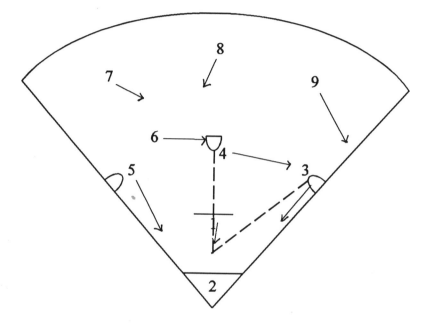

Runner on first base. Ball is bunted.

The pitcher, catcher, first or third baseman can field the ball with two hands and throw it to the second baseman covering first.

◆

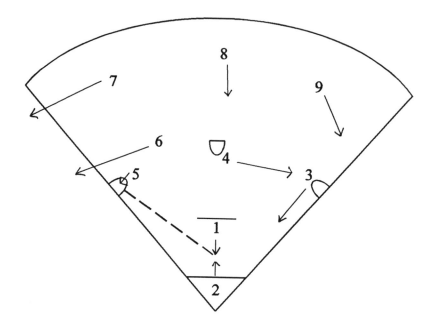

Runners on first and second base. Ball bunted to the pitcher, catcher or first baseman.

Field the ball and throw it to third for the force-out.

◆

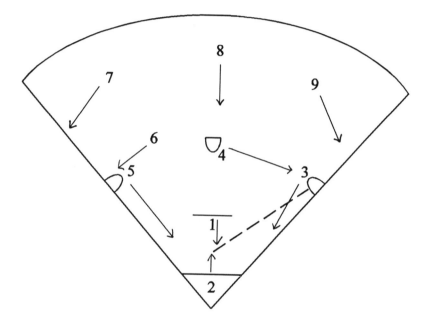

Runners on first and second base. Ball bunted to third, first, pitcher or catcher.

Field the ball and throw it to first base.

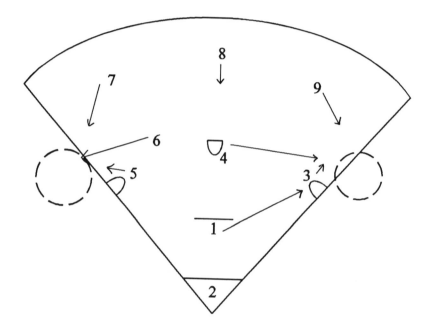

Fly ball hit out behind third or first base.

The shortstop should have priority on any fly balls, but especially in this area because he has a better angle than the third baseman to catch the ball.

The second baseman should have priority for the same reasons. The pitcher should cover any base left unoccupied.

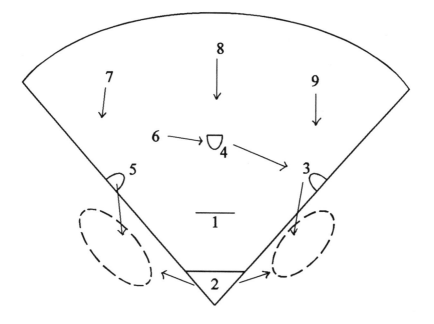

Fly ball hit to the catcher.

Practice communication between the third and first basemen on balls in foul territory.